# christinemanfield
# desserts

Christine Manfield is one of Australia's most celebrated chefs – a perfectionist inspired by strong flavours, and a writer whose succesful books, *Paramount Cooking*, *Spice* and *Stir*, have spiced up the lives of keen cooks from Melbourne to Manchester and Manhattan.

After working with some of Australia's best restaurateurs, in 1993 she opened the Paramount Restaurant in Sydney, which established her international reputation and was regarded as one of the finest in Australia by critics and the dining public alike. Since its closure at the end of 2000, she has broadened her global food interests, working alongside respected chefs around the world and hosting gastronomic tours to exotic destinations including Morocco, India, Spain and Turkey.

But Christine harboured 'a niggling restlessness to surrender to the demands of the kitchen again', and so when she was approached to create a new restaurant and lounge bar in London, she found it hard to resist. At East@West, in the heart of Soho, Christine is introducing Londoners to the unique kaleidoscope of Asian tastes and refined textures – inspired by the traditions and flavours of Vietnam, China and Japan – that have become her signature in Australia.

# christinemanfield
# desserts

photography by ashley barber

VIKING
*an imprint of*
PENGUIN BOOKS

Viking

Published by the Penguin Group (Australia)
250 Camberwell Road, Camberwell, Victoria 3124, Australia
Penguin Books Ltd
80 Strand, London WC2R 0RL, England
Penguin Group (USA) Inc.
375 Hudson Street, New York, New York 10014, USA
Penguin Books, a division of Pearson Canada
10 Alcorn Avenue, Toronto, Ontario, Canada M4V 3B2
Penguin Books (NZ) Ltd
Cnr Rosedale and Airborne Roads, Albany, Auckland, New Zealand
Penguin Books (South Africa) (Pty) Ltd
24 Sturdee Avenue, Rosebank, Johannesburg 2196, South Africa
Penguin Books India (P) Ltd
11, Community Centre, Panchsheel Park, New Delhi 110 017, India

First published as Paramount Desserts by
Penguin Books Australia Ltd, 1997
This paperback edition published by Penguin Books Australia,
a division of Pearson Australia Group, 2004

10 9 8 7 6 5 4 3 2 1

Cover design by Brad Maxwell © Penguin Group (Australia)
Text design by Jo Hunt © Penguin Group (Australia)
Author photograph by Jason Capobianco
Typeset in Gill Sans by Post Pre-press Group, Brisbane, Queensland
Printed in China by Imago

National Library of Australia
Cataloguing-in-Publication data:

Manfield, Christine.
Christine Manfield desserts.

Bibliography.
Includes index.
ISBN 0 670 04148 3.

1. Desserts. I. Title.

641.86

www.penguin.com.au

Front cover photograph: Chocolate Mocha Tart with
Espresso Ice-cream Cones (see page 44)
Back cover photograph: Passionfruit Miroir (see page 61)

NOTE The recipes in this collection generally serve six,
although some may yield slightly more.

**MY ADMIRATION AND DEEP APPRECIATION**

**GO TO THE PARAMOUNT DREAM TEAM**

for their relentless search for perfection

for their sense of purpose

for keeping the restaurant on track

for cooking brilliantly together

for chasing the same goals

for their commitment and dedication to the culinary arts

for their love of all things edible

for test-driving the recipes for this book

and for indulging me with the time to escape and write.

# FOREWORD

The Paramount Restaurant not only inspired chefs and foodies around Australia, but it also helped put Australia on the map as an international food destination.

My career in the Australian food industry started at the same time Chris Manfield and Margie Harris arrived in Sydney from Adelaide back in 1988. Their philosophy – the pursuit of excellence underpinned by passion, integrity, care and driving ambition – is something very dear to my heart. We are fortunate to have restaurateurs like Chris and Margie.

Following the success of the Paramount Restaurant, Chris's first book, *Paramount Cooking*, was published in 1995. This met with great critical acclaim and with three reprints in the first year was a publisher's dream! Now we can all enjoy *Christine Manfield Desserts*, which takes us on a culinary journey from the basics (far too often overlooked) to simple seasonal desserts and architectural masterpieces beautifully presented by leading Australian photographer Ashley Barber.

*Christine Manfield Desserts* is a must for anyone interested in the art of desserts. Whether you are looking for a recipe for a dinner party or are a professional in need of inspiration, this book delivers. Like everything Chris touches, its success comes back to her simple philosophy of being passionate about quality and her art. Be part of it.

SIMON JOHNSON
Simon Johnson Purveyor of Quality Foods

# CONTENTS

# INTRODUCTION

**D**essert gives pleasure, is food for the soul and is sensuous by its very nature. Never should dessert be seen as a flippant or excessive extra to any meal. It provides a vital structure and balance to a restaurant's menu, a meal and our diet and is intended to arouse passion and be provocative. At a restaurant or formal dinner, dessert is the final thing you eat. It leaves a lingering taste, a lasting impression.

I do not subscribe to the current paranoia that sugar is nasty: eating is about the art of balance, of feeding the mind and soul as well as the body. It is misinformed to think of dessert as excessive, indulgent or unnecessary. If you can't find room for dessert, it means you have ordered badly, eaten too much beforehand or not considered carefully enough the most appropriate progression of the meal. Dessert does not deserve this injustice! It needn't be consumed with every meal, but dessert certainly should play a prominent role when celebrating, cooking a special dinner for friends or eating in a restaurant. 'Sugar, of course', reports the Time-Life *Desserts* book, 'is present in practically any meal-ending creation. Most human beings have an irrepressible appetite for sweet things, and desserts exist to indulge it.'

The dessert portfolio on any serious restaurant menu is of paramount importance and, as far as I'm concerned, is an essential part of a chef's repertoire. Dessert-making challenges the chef like no other culinary discipline. It requires dedication, a true affinity with craft, artistry and creativity, and a solid understanding of the chemical processes involved in the assembly.

Having said that, dessert-making does not hold any hidden secrets or mysteries. It simply needs a flexible and sympathetic person who is prepared to acquire the skills to build confidence. Someone who has a sense of style.

The presentation of a dessert, and the use of flavours and textures, speaks volumes about personal style and integrity. The underlying philosophy and aesthetics of any restaurant should be reflected in the food offered, as should its 'personality' and reason for being. The responsibility of a good cook is to bring all the elements of a dish together – the parts have to make a whole – and each dish must be a force in its own right, a subliminal balancing of flavours and textures. Then each dessert has to work in competition with the others on the menu, the total of which should display an understanding of tastes and textures so that the list is neither repetitive nor one-dimensional.

The notion of dessert existing in its own right to provide a climax to a meal is a relatively new one. One of my sources of inspiration for decoration and spectacle is Antonin Carême (1783–1833), who incorporated architectural principles in his cooking in early nineteenth century France. Carême produced edible creations on a grand scale for the banquets of the rich, often using architectural drawings as a reference. At this time everything for a meal was laid on the table at the same time to create visual drama and provide a display of wealth and opulence. People ate haphazardly without regard or respect for the food, enjoying the architectural spectacle.

Author of several cookbooks, Carême established himself as the doyen of his profession at the time. His work was an expression of passion and dedication, something that remains entirely relevant and worthwhile today. Anne Willan quotes him in *Great Cooks and Their Recipes – from Taillevent to Escoffier* as expecting the ideal cook to 'have a discerning and sensitive palate, perfect and exquisite taste, strong and industrious character . . . be skilful and hardworking and unite delicacy, order and economy'. What more need be said?

The introduction of *à la russe* service in the latter part of the nineteenth century saw dessert being treated as a separate entity for the first time. Instead of being served as part of a banquet, as so artfully demonstrated by Carême, food appeared in a specific sequence. Then, in the early years of the twentieth century, Auguste Escoffier (1846–1935) introduced the practice of cooking individual *à la carte* portions to order. His *La Guide Culinaire* (1903), which offers standardised quantities and methods for professional use, is still a major reference for chefs and is used by restaurants to this day. 'It is to him', says Willan, 'that we owe the familiar shape of modern menus, many of our favourite dishes. Above all, it is Escoffier who finally put an end to the medieval principle of luxuriant display. After 500 years, quantity had at last surrendered to quality, and gluttony to gourmandise.' Suddenly people were offered a choice and the menu gave a meal a sense of reason and rhythm. This new approach allowed food to be cooked and served at its best and created a new art form for cooks to follow. Most importantly, perhaps, it saw dessert as completing a meal, something that by nature had to be tempting and inviting and that had to challenge all that had gone before it.

While France has produced two of the greatest dessert chefs to date, desserts and confectionery have a history and place in the cuisine of any culture, even if they have not been elevated to an art form or given sophisticated treatment. And some aren't served at the end of the meal, as is more usual in Western cultures. I have eaten sublime sweet nut pastries soaked with sugar and rosewater syrup in the Middle East and rich saffron-flavoured kulfi ice-cream and other milk confections in India. In Bali I had doll-doll, a favourite sweetmeat made with palm sugar and breadfruit and resembling a rich caramel toffee, and I have sampled the sweet coconut and rice confections available from carts on every Thai street corner. And then there are the divine and irresistible delicacies from the pâtisseries of Paris. Sugar comes in many guises and is there to tempt us regardless of time and place!

My aim with this body of work is to provide an insight into how my desserts are created and executed. I hope to give you an idea of the technique that has gone into creating these dishes, while also showing how flexibility can exist within such a disciplined field and how you, too, can become familiar with the laws of gravity, temperature and balance.

I set out with the deliberate intention to entice you, the reader, into the seductive, sensuous world of sugar and spice, the creations of which often play on sexual allusion and stimulate the mind and appetite in a healthy and positive way. Read and cook with desire, hunger and determination – mixing in a generous dose of time, patience, skill, passion and discipline – and see what you can come up with. Above all, have fun along the way!

# THE NECESSITIES

To make fabulous desserts, it is essential that the basics are thoroughly understood and that the cook is confident and in complete control. Dessert work, more than any other aspect of cooking, demands precision and close attention to detail for the best results. Flaws and mistakes are more difficult to hide and it is nearly impossible to make an intricate or complex dessert if the basics are faulty in the first place.

The recipes in this chapter form the foundation of the more elaborate and structural desserts that feature in the following chapters. It is not a comprehensive list of all basic recipes, but rather those that are used more than once in this book. Many of the recipes in this chapter stand alone in their own right and can be turned to when you want to serve something very simple with a piece of beautifully ripe fruit, or whatever. By working through these simple preparations, you will have an indispensable resource from which to draw when making more elaborate creations. Take command of these preparations and work with your imagination and skill – and experience the wonderful and enticing world of desserts.

While the quantities given here are small enough to work around the requirements needed for the recipes in this book, you may sometimes find yourself with a little left over. Use this as a start for something new, or just keep it as an instant snack.

# FRUIT SYRUPS AND SAUCES

**A** simple sugar syrup is an indispensable item to have on hand when making desserts. It can be made ahead of time and stored in the refrigerator until ready to use. Fruit syrups and sauces enhance the flavour of a dessert that is based on the same fruit.

## SUGAR SYRUP

1 litre water
1 kg castor sugar

1   Bring the water and castor sugar to a boil in a stainless steel saucepan. Simmer for 15 minutes, then remove from the heat and allow to cool.

2   Store the syrup in a bottle in the refrigerator until ready to use – it lasts almost indefinitely.

**Makes 1.25 litres**

## CITRUS SYRUP

3 limes, lemons, oranges *or*
    blood oranges
250 g castor sugar
50 ml water

This syrup can be made using any citrus fruit – I particularly like using either limes, lemons, oranges or blood oranges. Citrus syrup is great to have on hand to serve with fruit or ice-cream or to give added intensity to a dessert using the same flavour.

1   Zest and juice the fruit.

2   Bring the castor sugar and water to a boil in a saucepan and cook without stirring over a high heat until a pale caramel forms. Add the zest and juice and cook over a medium heat for a further 15 minutes until the mixture is syrupy.

3   Pour the syrup into a stainless steel bowl to stop the cooking process. Allow it to cool completely before using or refrigerating. The syrup keeps for about a month.

**Makes 300 ml**

## CHERRY SYRUP

200 ml Brandied Cherries liquid
    (see page 12)
100 ml Sugar Syrup (see above)

1   Bring the preserving liquid and sugar syrup to boiling point in a saucepan, then simmer over a medium heat until the liquid has reduced by half to become a syrup. Set aside

to cool until ready to use. The syrup keeps for about a month.

**Makes 150 ml**

# PASSIONFRUIT SYRUP

This syrup is wonderful to serve with fruit or ice-cream or to boost the passionfruit flavour in a dessert.

1   Bring the castor sugar and water to a boil in a stainless steel saucepan and cook without stirring over a high heat until a pale caramel forms. Add the passionfruit juice, then reduce the heat and simmer for 10 minutes. Remove the pan from the heat and stir in the pulp from the passionfruit.

2   Pour the syrup into a stainless steel bowl to stop the cooking process. Allow it to cool completely before using or refrigerating. The syrup keeps for about a month.

**Makes 500 ml**

300 g castor sugar
100 ml water
250 ml Passionfruit Juice (see page 10)
6 passionfruit

# QUINCE SYRUP

Flavour homemade vanilla or cinnamon ice-cream with this syrup, or spoon it over an apple tart or brioche. Try it with baked apples, quinces or pears, and serve it with cake and cream.

1   Chop the quinces coarsely, including the peel, core and seeds, then weigh them. Put the chopped quince into a large stainless steel stockpot with an equal weight of castor sugar, the cinnamon, the vanilla bean and enough water to cover the contents.

2   Bring the pot to a boil and cook over a medium heat for 2 hours or until the fruit is a dark and rich red and the liquid is syrupy.

3   Strain the syrup through a fine-meshed sieve or muslin into a bowl, pressing to extract as much liquid as possible. Discard the pulp. Cool the syrup, then refrigerate it until ready to use. The syrup keeps indefinitely.

**Makes 500 ml**

4 ripe quinces
castor sugar
1 stick cinnamon
1 vanilla bean, split

## PASSIONFRUIT JUICE

25 passionfruit

Passionfruit juice is not available in an instant form, so having frozen supplies to hand means you can achieve the intense flavour of the fruit without the presence of the seeds at any time of the year. Use passionfruit juice to flavour ice-cream, sorbet, cream, custard, a soufflé batter, syrup and so on. One ripe passionfruit yields about 10 ml or 2 teaspoons juice.

1   Cut the passionfruit in half and remove the pulp with a spoon, then press the pulp through a fine-meshed sieve into a bowl, squeezing out as much juice as possible. Discard the seeds.

2   If you are not using the juice immediately, freeze it in small amounts for later use.

**Makes 250 ml**

## RASPBERRY SAUCE

500 g raspberries
100 ml Sugar Syrup (see page 8)
25 ml strained fresh lemon juice

1   Purée the raspberries with the sugar syrup and lemon juice in a food processor or blender. Pass the purée through a fine-meshed sieve and discard the seeds.

2   Store the sauce in the refrigerator and use it within 3 days or the fruit will start to separate from the sugar. Whisk the sauce again just as you are about to serve it.

**Makes 300 ml**

## STRAWBERRY SAUCE

500 g ripe strawberries, hulled
125 g castor sugar
25 ml strained fresh lemon juice

1   Purée the strawberries with the castor sugar and lemon juice in a food processor or blender. Pass the purée through a fine-meshed sieve and discard the seeds.

2   Store the sauce in the refrigerator and use it within 3 days or the fruit will start to separate from the sugar. Whisk the sauce again just as you are about to serve it.

**Makes 300 ml**

# POACHED AND PRESERVED FRUIT

The ritual of preserving fruit is an important one in any serious cook's life. Preserving makes the most of the perfect ripeness, perfume and flavour of fruit, and time, patience and imagination are essential ingredients in the process. For further reading and inspiration, refer to *Jane Grigson's Fruit Book* – it's packed with information and wonderful ideas that supersede fashion and vacuous trends.

I prefer to poach fruit in a single layer in a heavy-based pan that is as wide as possible. The one I use is about 40 cm wide and 20 cm deep. The base of the pan must have equal access to heat so that the fruit doesn't stew. If you don't have such a pan, try a heavy-based baking dish or poach the fruit in batches in your largest saucepan.

## POACHED QUINCES

Quinces come into season at the end of summer and are available for about three months. The ripe fruit has a heavenly musky aroma that perfumes the refrigerator or room in which it is stored. But because of their less-than-appealing raw state and the fact that they need long, careful cooking to bring out their unique flavour and texture, quinces are often overlooked.

While quinces can be cooked with meat as is done in Tunisia and Morocco, I prefer to use them in desserts. Their uses are many and varied: I give marmalade and jelly recipes in *Paramount Cooking* and incorporate both in desserts, as I do these poached quinces and the Quince Syrup on page 9. Try filling a tart shell with cream and adding poached quinces, or simply serve the fruit with custard.

For detailed information about the quince, read *The Cook's Companion*, Stephanie Alexander's brilliant reference book, which is indispensable in any kitchen.

3 litres water
2 kg castor sugar
2 star anise
1 stick cinnamon
2 cloves
1 lemon, thickly sliced
6 ripe quinces

1   Preheat the oven to 150°C. Put the water, castor sugar, spices and lemon into a wide, heavy-based pan and bring to a boil on the stove, then reduce the heat to a mere simmer.

2   Peel the quinces and cut them in half lengthwise, leaving their cores and seeds intact. Put the quinces into the simmering liquid, then press a sheet of baking paper down onto the fruit and cover the pan with a lid or secure it tightly with a double sheet of foil. Gently poach the fruit in the oven for 7–8 hours until soft and red.

3   Using a slotted spoon, carefully remove the fruit from the syrup and put it into 3 x 2 litre hot, sterilised preserving jars. Strain the syrup and pour it over the fruit to cover. Seal the jars and store in the refrigerator until ready to use. The quinces will keep in perfect condition for 3–4 months. As you need to use the fruit, remove it from the syrup and cut away the core and seeds before serving.

**Makes 6 litres**

## BRANDIED PEACHES

750 ml sauternes
250 ml riesling
1 litre Sugar Syrup (see page 8)
1 vanilla bean, split
16 ripe slipstone peaches,
    washed
750 ml brandy

1   Bring the sauternes, riesling, sugar syrup and vanilla bean to a boil in a wide, heavy-based pan, then boil gently for 30 minutes.

2   Reduce the heat to low, then add the peaches in a single layer and poach very gently for 10 minutes, turning them regularly in the liquid. Remove the peaches from the syrup and allow them to cool enough to handle, then peel.

3   Add the brandy to the syrup and remove the vanilla bean. Divide the peaches between 2 x 2 litre hot, sterilised preserving jars and pour in the hot syrup until the peaches are covered, then seal. Label and store the jars until ready to use. The peaches keep well, refrigerated, for a few months.

**Makes 4 litres**

## BRANDIED CHERRIES

2 kg sweet cherries
1 litre Sugar Syrup (see page 8)
1 stick cinnamon
1 vanilla bean, split
3 whole mace
300 ml cherry brandy
100 ml brandy

Cherries have such a short season in summer that it seems criminal not to make the most of their flavour and extend their life beyond what nature allows. Preserving gives you the opportunity to dwell on the taste longer, to use the fruit out of season. It also increases your options when planning what dessert to serve, so have the forethought to stock up your pantry with the season's abundance.

1   Stone the cherries and remove their stems.

2   Bring all the ingredients except the cherries to a boil in a wide, heavy-based saucepan and simmer for 30 minutes. Discard the mace, vanilla bean and cinnamon stick.

3   Add the cherries and simmer gently for 15 minutes, stirring occasionally. Spoon the cherries and their syrup into 3 x 1 litre hot, sterilised preserving jars and seal. Label and store the jars until ready to use. The cherries keep well, refrigerated, for a few months.

**Makes 3 litres**

# MUSCAT-POACHED FRUIT

Other than the uses to which I put muscat-poached fruit in 'Architectural Offerings' and *Paramount Cooking*, it can be eaten cold with clotted cream and a sprinkle of praline or it can fill a baked tart shell lined with cream or mascarpone. Try gently heating the fruit and serving it with brioche, cake or fruit toast, too.

Dried fruit gives you the chance to make a fruit dessert in winter when supplies of fresh produce are limited. Choose fruit that has been recently dried and is soft, malleable and fresh tasting.

750 ml liqueur muscat
250 ml water
500 g castor sugar
1 vanilla bean, split
75 ml vanilla essence
10 dried figs, halved
12 dried apricots
10 dried peaches, halved
8 prunes, stoned
5 dried pineapple rings, quartered
100 g dried cherries

1   In a wide, heavy-based saucepan, bring the muscat, water, castor sugar, vanilla bean and vanilla essence to a boil over a high heat and simmer for 20 minutes until the liquid begins to thicken and become syrupy.

2   Reduce the heat to low and add all the fruit. Simmer for 20 minutes until the fruit is tender and the syrup has reduced slightly. Stir regularly to distribute the fruit evenly in the syrup. Spoon the fruit and its syrup into 2 x 1 litre hot, sterilised preserving jars and seal. Label and store the jars until ready to use. The fruit keeps well, refrigerated, for several months.

**Makes 2 litres**

# TOFFEE APPLE

These apple slices are baked briefly in caramel, which gives them a luscious toffee coating. They can then be baked into a tart, brioche or cake without throwing moisture into the dough or batter during cooking.

6 golden delicious apples
butter
100 ml water
500 g castor sugar

1   Preheat the oven to 200°C. Peel and core the apples and cut them into eighths lengthwise. Butter a baking dish and arrange the apple slices in a single layer over the base.

2   Bring the water and castor sugar to a boil in a saucepan without stirring and cook over a high heat until a caramel forms, then pour this over the apple.

3   Bake the apple in the oven for 7 minutes, then turn the slices over and cook for a further 5 minutes. Remove the apple from the baking dish while still warm and store on a sheet of baking paper until ready to use. Pour some of the caramel over the apple to keep it moist, and use within the day.

# CUMQUAT MARMALADE

2 kg cumquats, washed
castor sugar

Try adding this marmalade to a tart with a ginger or orange custard, baking it in brioche or spooning it between layers of puff pastry with vanilla cream. I also use it instead of brandied cherries in the cherry almond cake that appears in *Paramount Cooking*.

1  Cut the cumquats in half and remove the seeds. Tie the seeds in a piece of muslin.

2  Weigh the cumquats and put them into a bucket and cover with water. Leave in the refrigerator overnight.

3  Put the cumquats, their soaking water and the seeds into a heavy-based stockpot and add castor sugar to half the weight of the cumquats. Bring the pot to a boil, then simmer for 1 hour. Turn off the heat, then cover the pot and allow it to stand overnight.

4  Next day, bring the pot to a boil again and cook the marmalade until it reaches 110°C or setting point. Remove the bag of seeds and ladle the marmalade into hot, sterilised jars and seal.

**Makes 2 litres**

# CREAMS, CUSTARDS AND MERINGUE

Creams and custards are the epitome of smoothness, richness and gentle sweetness. Their texture varies depending on how they are cooked, whether they are stirred to the desired thickness over a bain-marie or baked in a water bath until firm. It is the magical chemistry between eggs, sugar and cream or milk that produces these wonderful taste sensations.

Equally intriguing is the magic that egg whites create when beaten with sugar to make a meringue: a mixture of apparently no substance produces fragile confections of great beauty with the application of gentle heat.

## MERINGUE

1   Whip the egg whites until stiff peaks form, then slowly add the castor sugar, still whisking, to make a stiff meringue.

2   Sift the icing sugar and cornflour together and fold into the meringue.

3   Proceed with the recipe you are following. If you just want to make small meringues, pipe little peaked drops of the mixture onto a baking tray lined with baking paper and cook at 50°C for 1 hour. Cool the meringues on a wire rack for 30 minutes, then store in an airtight container until ready to use.

100 g egg whites
100 g castor sugar
100 g icing sugar
15 g cornflour

## LEMON CURD

Lemon curd or butter reminds us of good home cooking, afternoon teas, and fêtes and fairs, where it is found in jars with handwritten labels, much like a favourite jam. Grandmothers always seem to pass on a recipe for lemon curd, such is its popularity! It is an essential element of a lemon meringue pie, but it can be used in various ways: on toast, in a sponge – just use your imagination! A necessary and delectable item to have in the refrigerator.

5 large egg yolks
100 g castor sugar
110 ml strained fresh lemon juice
125 g unsalted butter

1   Whisk the egg yolks and castor sugar in a bowl until light and fluffy. Add the lemon juice, then stand the bowl over a bain-marie and cook until thick, stirring constantly.

2   Add the butter piece by piece, allowing each piece to incorporate before stirring in the next. The mixture should have become thicker by the time the last piece of butter has been added. Remove the bowl from the heat and stand it over ice to cool. Store the curd in a sealed container in the refrigerator.

**Makes 350 ml**

# VANILLA MASCARPONE

2 limes
1 litre pouring (35 per cent) cream
1 vanilla bean, split and scraped
1 scant teaspoon citric acid

1   Zest and juice the limes.

2   Bring the lime zest, cream and vanilla bean to a vigorous boil in a deep stainless steel saucepan. Boil for 5 minutes until the cream separates.

3   Add the lime juice and citric acid to the cream mixture and bring it back to a boil. Simmer for 1 minute, then remove from the heat. Pour the cream through a fine-meshed sieve or muslin into a bowl. Put the bowl into the refrigerator until the mixture starts to set, about 5 hours.

4   Line a conical sieve with a double layer of wet muslin and position it over a 2 litre plastic container. Pour the set cream into the sieve, then cover with plastic film and let it stand for 24 hours in the refrigerator to allow the whey to separate from the curd.

5   Discard the whey and scoop the mascarpone from the sieve into a plastic container, then seal and refrigerate until ready to use. The vanilla mascarpone will keep, refrigerated, for a week.

**Makes 700 g**

# THICK VANILLA CREAM

700 ml thick (45 per cent) cream
2 vanilla beans, split
12 large egg yolks
100 g castor sugar

1   Put the cream into a saucepan and scrape in the seeds from the vanilla bean. Bring to simmering point over a low heat.

2   Whisk the egg yolks and castor sugar in a bowl, then gently pour in the hot cream and stir well. Cook the mixture gently over a bain-marie, stirring, until the consistency of a thick custard – be careful that the mixture does not overcook and become granular.

3   Whisk the custard over ice to cool. Press plastic film over the surface of the custard to prevent a skin forming and refrigerate until set. Vanilla cream will keep, refrigerated, for 3 days if you want to make it ahead of time.

**Makes 900 ml**

# VANILLA CUSTARD

Nothing comes near perfectly made vanilla custard (it is also known by its French name *crème anglaise*, but I think it's pretentious to use such terms in an Australian context). This stirred custard is the real thing: it bears no relationship to processed preparations for instant use. It has a soft texture and can be served hot or cold.

250 ml milk
500 ml pouring (35 per cent) cream
1 vanilla bean, split
8 egg yolks
150 g castor sugar

1   Bring the milk, cream and vanilla bean to simmering point in a saucepan over low heat.

2   Whisk the egg yolks and castor sugar in a bowl until pale and creamy. Whisk the hot milk mixture and the vanilla bean into the egg mixture to incorporate. Stand the bowl over a bain-marie and stir over a gentle heat until the desired consistency is reached. Remove the bowl from the heat and pass the custard through a fine-meshed sieve into a clean bowl, then discard the vanilla bean.

3   Serve the custard immediately unless you are making it ahead of time. In this case, store it in the refrigerator with plastic film pressed down onto the surface to prevent a skin forming. To serve, gently reheat the custard in a bowl over a bain-marie, whisking to keep it smooth and aerated.

**Makes 800 ml**

# CHOCOLATE CREAM

This preparation is also known as chocolate ganache – it is a vital confection that has a myriad uses, as you will discover as you familiarise yourself with the chocolate recipes in this book. Once made, the mixture usually needs to cool before you can work with it effectively.

250 g dark couverture chocolate
200 ml thick (45 per cent) cream

1   Shave the chocolate into a bowl.

2   Heat the cream to simmering point and pour it over the chocolate. Stir until combined and glossy.

3   If using the chocolate cream to ice a cake, do so while it is liquid. The mixture will become firm when stored in the refrigerator, making it suitable for use as a filling or to make chocolate truffles.

**Makes 350 ml**

# BISCUITS AND WAFERS

These fragile structures add an ethereal element to desserts – they often contain or envelop a secret centre and seem solid but dissolve on the tongue after their initial crunch, providing textural complexity.

## TUILE BISCUITS

50 g unsalted butter
50 g castor sugar
2 egg whites
50 g plain flour

Apart from the specific uses to which they are put in the 'Architectural Offerings' chapter, these biscuits can be served with ice-cream, fruit or custards, or with coffee or tea as a petit four; they can also be moulded into cones and filled with sorbet.

The mixture for these biscuits will keep in an airtight container in the refrigerator for two weeks, so make as much as you need and keep the remainder for further use. If you follow the applications in 'Architectural Offerings', you should achieve up to twenty biscuits.

1   Cream the butter and castor sugar in an electric mixer until pale and creamy. This will take up to 10 minutes.

2   Fold the unbeaten egg whites into the mixture a little at a time. Add the flour and work until the dough becomes smooth. (If you are making the mixture ahead of time, this is the point to refrigerate it in an airtight container.)

3   Work the mixture while it is soft and pliable. (If you have refrigerated the mixture, let it come to room temperature before working with it.) With a palette knife, spread a thin layer of the mixture onto a buttered and floured 30 cm x 24 cm baking tray. Put the tray into the refrigerator until the mixture becomes firm, about 1 hour. This prevents the biscuits from fracturing during cooking.

4   Preheat the oven to 160°C and bake the chilled mixture for 4 minutes, then remove from the heat. The mixture should be just set but not cooked or coloured. Using a sharp knife, quickly cut biscuits to your desired shape, depending on the specifications of the recipe, then remove the unwanted mixture and return the tray to the oven for 3 minutes. The biscuits should now be cooked and pale golden brown. Remove the tray from the oven and slide the biscuits onto a wire rack to set. Store in an airtight container until ready to use.

# BRANDY SNAP BISCUITS

These biscuits can be served in the same way as the tuiles (see page 18) and give added texture to a dessert. The mixture keeps perfectly in the refrigerator for a month. It becomes hard when cold so needs to be brought back to room temperature before being used, where it will become pliable and easy to handle. As with the tuiles, the yield will depend on the size of the biscuits, but expect to achieve about twenty when making any of the 'Architectural Offerings' preparations.

100 g unsalted butter
90 g liquid glucose
180 g castor sugar
90 g plain flour

1    Melt the butter and liquid glucose in a bowl over a bain-marie. Mix the castor sugar and flour in another bowl, then pour in the melted butter and glucose and stir to incorporate. Allow to cool before proceeding. Refrigerate the mixture in an airtight container at this stage if making it ahead of time.

2    Preheat the oven to 180°C and line 2 baking trays with baking paper. Roll the mixture into small balls, using a teaspoonful for each. Cook 2 biscuits at a time on a baking tray, well spaced, for 5 minutes or until caramel-coloured. Remove the tray from the oven, then allow the biscuits to cool for 15–20 seconds. While warm and pliable, cut each biscuit into rounds using a pastry cutter (unless otherwise specified, use an 8 cm pastry cutter). Allow the biscuits to cool and firm on the tray, then transfer them to an airtight container until ready to use. Cook another 2 biscuits on the second baking tray to keep the process going while one batch cools.

# LEMON SHORTBREAD BISCUITS

These biscuits are made from the same dough as the Shortbread Pastry later in this chapter, but include lemon zest and juice. Other citrus peel such as orange, grapefruit or lime can be substituted to give a different flavour, as can minced candied ginger. An 8 cm pastry cutter will give you eighteen biscuits, while a 4 cm one will yield thirty-six.

1 quantity Shortbread Pastry
   dough (see page 23)
½ teaspoon fresh lemon juice
2 teaspoons minced lemon zest
icing sugar

1    Make the dough as instructed, working the lemon juice and zest in when you add the egg yolks. Wrap the dough in plastic film and rest it in the refrigerator for at least 2 hours before rolling.

2    Roll the dough out on a cool, floured surface to about 5 mm thick, then cut it into the desired shapes. Refrigerate the dough for 30 minutes before baking.

3    Preheat the oven to 150°C. Bake the biscuits for 6 minutes until firm but not coloured, then slide them onto a wire rack to firm up and cool. Store the cooled biscuits in an airtight container between layers of baking paper until ready to use. Dust with icing sugar to serve.

# PASTRY

The making of pastry is an integral part of the dessert repertoire and a therapeutic and rewarding practice. Even though pastry can be fickle and difficult, patience, care and perseverance will win out as you develop a deft hand and a feel for and understanding of the process.

As with all cooking, often the best way to understand a procedure properly is to have a few failures along the way. More can be learnt from mistakes than if you fluke it, as failure forces you to examine the whys and hows. So never despair: just turn around and have another go. It's like falling off a bike: the best thing for your esteem and confidence is to start again and prove you can do it.

One of the most important factors in making a successful pastry is temperature. Pastry responds best in a cool, humidity-free environment, preferably below 18°C. Working the ingredients for short intervals and resting the pastry in the refrigerator between each step helps maintain the correct temperature.

The quality of the ingredients used bears a direct relationship to the flavour and the texture of the finished pastry. Unsalted butter is used as it is a fresher product; salt is added by the cook as required. Other fats such as margarine have a different fat-molecule structure and may give a different result. If time is of the essence, pastry can be prepared ahead, rolled and frozen until ready to use. Just allow it to defrost in the refrigerator before baking.

## PUFF PASTRY

500 g plain flour
1 teaspoon sea salt
½ teaspoon fresh lemon juice
250 ml mineral water, chilled
500 g unsalted butter, chilled
1 egg yolk

The nature of puff pastry lies in its preparation, where layers of butter and flour are multiplied through repeated folding and rolling. With the application of heat, the air that has been trapped between the layers expands and the water evaporates, causing the layers to separate and push up.

Puff pastry is the most complicated of all pastries: the temperature at which it is made is as important as the resting time between turns, and the rolling of the dough must be carried out without breaking the surface, which will allow the all-important butter to escape. That said, making puff pastry is a most rewarding and satisfying exercise – an art form that should not be lost in today's hurried world, where such skills are disappearing rapidly. Machine-made, processed goods simply do not replace the pleasures of making or eating this pastry.

Puff pastry is best made the day it is needed as it deflates when stored – any leftovers freeze well.

1   Chill the bowl and blade of a food processor in the refrigerator.

2   Blend the flour, salt, lemon juice and mineral water in the food processor until homogenous. Refrigerate the pastry in the food processor bowl for 1 hour.

3   Work the cold dough in the food processor a second time but for a minute only; this works the glutens, giving elasticity and preventing shrinkage. Wrap the dough in plastic film, making sure it is airtight. Rest for 1 hour in the refrigerator.

4   Roll the dough out on a flat, cold surface to make a 40 cm × 30 cm rectangle about 1 cm thick. Position the dough so that the longest side is facing you.

5   Cut the cold butter into 1 cm thick slices and arrange in a single layer down the middle of the rectangle of dough. (It is important that the dough and the butter are of the same temperature and equal thickness to give uniformity to the layers when rolling.) Fold in the edges of the dough to encase the butter. Flatten the dough with a rolling pin, then dust it with flour and refrigerate for 30 minutes, wrapped in plastic film.

6   Each time you work the pastry, dust it with flour and work on a cool surface. Using even pressure, roll the dough until it is 90 cm × 40 cm with the longest side facing you. Fold the dough over 3 times to end up with a piece that is 30 cm × 40 cm. Turn the dough to your right and repeat the rolling and folding process, continuing until you have turned the dough twice.

7   Rest the dough in the refrigerator for 1 hour. (It is important to rest the dough at these intervals to prevent it from heating and to inhibit the glutens from building up through overworking.)

8   Continue the rolling and turning process until you have made 6 turns, refrigerating the dough for 1 hour after every second turn.

9   After the final resting, roll the dough out until 1 cm thick. Cut the dough into the desired shape, then brush the surface with the egg yolk, being careful not to let any drip down the sides (this will prevent even rising). Allow the pastry to firm again in the refrigerator for 30 minutes before baking.

10   Score the top of the pastry with a sharp knife, if desired, and bake as required by your recipe (12 minutes at 180°C is a general cooking time).

11   Cool the cooked pastry on a wire rack and store it in an airtight container if not using it immediately. Best used on the day it is made, puff pastry can be reheated in a 160°C oven for 4 minutes.

## SWEET PASTRY

80 g icing sugar
125 g plain flour
75 g unsalted butter
2 egg yolks
½ vanilla bean, split

When sugar is used in pastry-making, it produces a crisp result similar to but more fragile than a savoury shortcrust pastry. The following sweet pastry (also known as *pâte sucrée*) is a versatile one for dessert work. This quantity of pastry is sufficient for six 12 cm tarts or a 24 cm one.

1   Chill the bowl and blade of a food processor in the refrigerator.

2   Sift the icing sugar and flour and incorporate with the butter in the food processor until the mixture resembles fine breadcrumbs.

3   Add the egg yolks to the flour and butter and scrape in the seeds from the vanilla bean. Blend until the dough just comes together. Wrap the dough in plastic film and refrigerate for 2 hours.

4   Roll out the pastry on a cold, floured surface until 5 mm thick, then cut it into the shape required by your recipe and line your chosen flan tin or tins (grease the tin with butter if it is not non-stick). Refrigerate the pastry for 30 minutes before baking.

5   Preheat the oven to 160°C. Blind bake the tart shell or shells until crisp and pale golden. The timing will depend on the size of the tin you are using. Small tart shells take 11 minutes, while a larger one will take about 18 minutes.

## SWEET ORANGE PASTRY

125 g unsalted butter, diced and chilled
90 g icing sugar
1 teaspoon minced orange zest
1 egg
½ teaspoon orange essence *or* orange-flower water
250 g plain flour

Orange essence is available from speciality shops, but orange-flower water can also be used. This quantity of pastry is sufficient for six 12 cm tart shells or a 30 cm one.

1   Chill the bowl and blade of a food processor in the refrigerator.

2   Blend the butter, icing sugar and orange zest together to make a smooth paste, then add the egg and orange essence. Add the flour and pulse just until the dough comes together. Remove the dough from the bowl, then wrap it in plastic film and refrigerate for 2 hours.

3   Roll out the pastry on a cold, floured surface until 5 mm thick, then cut it into the shape required by your recipe and line your chosen flan tin or tins (butter the tin first if it is not non-stick). Refrigerate the pastry for 30 minutes before baking.

4   Preheat the oven to 160°C. Blind bake the tart shell or shells until crisp and pale golden. The timing will depend on the size of the tin you are using. Small tart shells take· 11 minutes and a larger tart shell will take about 18 minutes.

# SWEET LEMON PASTRY

This quantity of pastry is sufficient for six 12 cm tart shells or a 30 cm one.

1   Chill the bowl and blade of a food processor in the refrigerator.

2   Sift the flour and icing sugar and then blend with the lemon zest in the food processor. With the motor running, scrape in the seeds from the vanilla bean and add the butter, egg and lemon juice and work until the dough forms a ball. Wrap the dough in plastic film and refrigerate for 2 hours.

3   Roll out the pastry on a cold, floured surface until 5 mm thick, then cut it into the shape required by your recipe and line your chosen flan tin or tins (butter the tin first if it is not non-stick). Refrigerate the pastry for 30 minutes before baking.

4   Preheat the oven to 160°C. Blind bake the tart shell or shells until crisp and pale golden. The timing will depend on the size of the tin you are using. Small tart shells take 11 minutes and a larger tart shell will take about 18 minutes.

275 g plain flour
90 g icing sugar
½ teaspoon minced lemon zest
½ vanilla bean, split
125 g unsalted butter, diced and chilled
1 egg
20 ml fresh lemon juice

# SHORTBREAD PASTRY

A higher ratio of fat to flour produces a shorter pastry that is harder to handle and softer in texture than those with more flour. This pastry (also known as sablé) is fragile and is at its best served fresh since it is highly perishable. It can be used to make a 20 cm tart shell (or six 12 cm tarts) or about twenty biscuits.

1   Chill the bowl and blade of a food processor in the refrigerator.

2   Cream the butter in the food processor until soft. Sift in the icing sugar and work until thoroughly blended. Add the egg yolk and vanilla essence and mix lightly. Sift in the flour and pulse until the dough just comes together. Wrap the dough in plastic film and refrigerate for at least 2 hours.

3   Roll out the pastry on a cold, floured surface until 5 mm thick, then cut it into the shape required by your recipe and line a flan tin (butter the tin first if it is not non-stick) or cut it into biscuit shapes using a round or fluted pastry cutter. If making a tart, prick the base of the pastry with a fork to prevent shrinkage during cooking (this avoids having to blind bake later). Refrigerate the pastry for 30 minutes before baking.

4   If making a tart, the cooking time will depend on the size of the tin you are using. Small tart shells take 11 minutes at 160°C, while a larger one will take about 18 minutes. Don't worry if the tart shell fractures – just patch it up with some of the pastry in the tin.

5   If making biscuits, bake at 150°C for 6 minutes until firm but not coloured. Dust the cooled biscuits with icing sugar to serve.

100 g unsalted butter
90 g icing sugar
1 egg yolk
½ teaspoon vanilla essence
140 g plain flour

# CHOCOLATE PASTRY

125 g unsalted butter, softened
125 g castor sugar
1 teaspoon vanilla essence
150 g plain flour
50 g Dutch cocoa powder

This is my slightly amended version of a fabulous pastry from one of Australia's most celebrated chefs and culinary writers, Stephanie Alexander. It is like a chocolate short-bread, very moist with a fine crumb, and is used as a base for the Chocolate Mocha Tart (see page 44). It can also be used for other chocolate fillings, such as chocolate mousse, bavarois or butter cream. I have also suggested it as an alternative base for the Lemon Curd Tarts (see page 80). This is one pastry I use immediately after I have made it. I don't refrigerate it before lining the tin and nor do I roll it, since its crumbly texture makes this difficult.

1   Cream the butter and the castor sugar in an electric mixer until pale, then mix in the vanilla essence.

2   Sift the flour and cocoa powder together and incorporate into the butter mixture until a dough has formed – it will feel quite wet.

3   Grease a 24 cm fluted flan tin, preferably one with a removable base, and press the dough into the sides and over the base with your fingertips, ensuring the pastry is evenly distributed. Rest the pastry in the refrigerator for 1 hour.

4   Preheat the oven to 180°C and bake the tart shell for 10 minutes. The pastry will bubble up slightly and slip down the sides a little, so when you take the tart shell out of the oven press the pastry back into its original shape using a clean tea towel while it is still hot and malleable. Work quickly because once the pastry cools it holds its shape.

# CRÈME FRAÎCHE FLAKY PASTRY

The flakiness and richness of this pastry is due to the high ratio of fat to flour. Because it is so short, it is best used for pies with dry fillings and is not recommended for tart cases, as it will crumble. This is one pastry I don't recommend freezing – it's best made and used immediately. This quantity is sufficient for one large or a dozen small pies.

Although I don't use this pastry in any of the preparations in this book, I include it here as it is a useful one with which to be familiar. It can be successfully substituted for the puff pastry used in the recipe for fig and blue cheese pastries on page 54.

125 g unsalted butter, chilled
200 g plain flour
90 g icing sugar
½ teaspoon sea salt
125 g crème fraîche, chilled
1 egg yolk

1   Chill the bowl and blade of a food processor in the refrigerator.

2   Chop the butter into chunks and, while still cold, blend with the flour, icing sugar and salt in the food processor until the mixture resembles breadcrumbs.

3   Add the crème fraîche and pulse until just incorporated. Don't overwork the mixture at this stage or the pastry will be quite difficult to handle when rolling. Work the pastry into a ball by hand, then wrap it in plastic film and refrigerate for 2 hours.

4   Roll out and cut the pastry according to the recipe you are following, being careful that the pastry remains cool and stays reasonably firm as you do so. If you want to make small pies, use a 10 cm pastry cutter for the bases and an 8 cm one for the lids. Work quickly in small batches, otherwise you may have difficulty in achieving the desired result. (If you are making a large pie, cut the pastry in half and roll out each piece to make the base and then the lid.) Refrigerate the pastry for 30 minutes (if making a large pie, line a pie dish with the pastry before refrigerating it).

5   Brush the pastry bases with egg yolk, then fill the pies according to your recipe. Cover with the pastry lids, then press the edges together with your fingers and smooth them with a paring knife. Brush the lids with egg yolk and, if desired, score 6 arcs around the dome of each, working from the top down. Refrigerate the pies for 1 hour before baking.

6   Preheat the oven to 180°C. Bake small pies for 15 minutes. A large pie will need 15 minutes at 180°C, then another 15 minutes at 150°C.

# BRIOCHES AND CAKES

While Marie-Antoinette is reported to have said 'Let them eat cake!' when complaining about peasants uprising against a lack of bread in eighteenth century Paris, the 'cake' was in fact brioche – 'Qu'ils mangent de la brioche!'.

Brioches and cakes are essential components of a dessert repertoire. Cakes are made from sweet batters that have many different formulae, structures and methods of preparation. Brioches are made light with the addition of yeast, are enriched with butter and eggs and are worked and kneaded in a similar fashion to bread dough. Although I include only a handful of recipes here, they can be used and adapted to give many different results.

## BUTTER BRIOCHE

250 g plain flour
pinch of sea salt
50 g castor sugar
15 g fresh yeast
50 ml warm milk
3 large eggs
250 g unsalted butter, softened

Brioche dough is beaten until it becomes very elastic and shiny and can be used to encase savoury or sweet fillings. This quantity of dough will make nine small brioches. It can also be baked as a 24 cm x 10 cm x 10 cm loaf. Try it for breakfast as toast – a luscious alternative to bread!

1   Combine the flour, salt and 25 g of the castor sugar in the bowl of an electric mixer fitted with a dough hook. In another bowl, mix the yeast with the warm milk and the remaining sugar. Whisk the eggs in another bowl again.

2   Incorporate the yeast mixture into the flour with a dough hook on low speed. Add the eggs and turn the speed to high. Mix for 5 minutes or until the dough appears elastic. With the dough hook still on high speed, add the butter in small chunks until the dough has combined and is smooth and shiny.

3   Put the dough into a greased bowl and cover it with plastic film. Let it rise in a warm place for about 45 minutes or until it has doubled in size.

4   Punch the dough down and roll or knead it into the desired shape. Butter and sugar the chosen moulds and put the brioche dough into them. Allow the brioche to rise again for 30 minutes.

5   Preheat the oven to 190°C. Bake the brioche over a water bath until golden. Small brioches will take 12 minutes, while a large loaf will take 20–25 minutes. Allow the brioche to cool slightly, then turn out onto a wire rack to cool completely. If serving immediately, remove the brioche from the mould or moulds while still hot.

# CINNAMON BRIOCHE

This quantity of dough will make six small brioches or a 24 cm x 10 cm x 10 cm loaf.

1   Combine the flour, 25 g of the castor sugar, the cinnamon and the salt in the bowl of an electric mixer fitted with a dough hook. In another bowl, mix the yeast into the warm milk with the remaining sugar. Whisk the eggs in another bowl again.

2   Incorporate the yeast mixture into the flour with a dough hook on low speed. Add the eggs and turn the speed to high. Mix for 5 minutes or until the dough appears elastic. With the dough hook still on high speed, add the butter in small chunks until the dough has combined and is smooth and shiny.

3   Put the dough into a greased bowl and cover it with plastic film. Let it rise in a warm place for about 45 minutes or until it has doubled in size.

4   Punch the dough down and roll or knead into the desired shape. Butter and sugar the chosen moulds and put the brioche dough into them. Allow the brioche to rise again for 30 minutes.

5   Preheat the oven to 190°C. Bake the brioche over a water bath until golden. Small brioches will take 12 minutes, while a large loaf will take 20–25 minutes. Allow the brioche to cool slightly, then turn out onto a wire rack to cool completely. If serving immediately, remove the brioche from the mould or moulds while still hot.

250 g plain flour
50 g castor sugar
1 tablespoon ground cinnamon
pinch of sea salt
10 g fresh yeast
50 ml warm milk
2 large eggs
150 g unsalted butter, softened

# GÉNOISE SPONGE

1   Preheat the oven to 160°C and grease and line a 24 cm square cake tin.

2   Whisk the egg yolks and castor sugar in a bowl until pale and creamy. Add the flour, vanilla essence and the cooled melted butter and stir to incorporate.

3   Whip the egg whites until stiff peaks form, then fold them gently into the cake batter with a spatula. Pour the batter into the prepared cake tin and bake for 20 minutes or until cooked. Test by inserting a skewer into the centre – if it comes out clean, the cake is cooked. Turn out onto a wire rack to cool.

5 large eggs, separated
150 g castor sugar
150 g plain flour, sifted
1 teaspoon vanilla essence
50 g unsalted butter, melted

# CHOCOLATE FUDGE CAKE

100 g dark couverture chocolate
100 g unsalted butter
3 large eggs, separated
150 g castor sugar
50 g plain flour, sifted

The quantities for this cake can easily be doubled, tripled or whatever. The cooking time will remain relatively the same if the depth of the tin is constant – just make sure the tin is wider rather than deeper when making a larger batch of batter. This cake is baked with a water bath on the shelf below to ensure gentle, moist cooking.

1   Preheat the oven to 160°C and grease and line a 30 cm x 24 cm cake tin that is 5 cm deep. Shave the chocolate into a bowl and melt it gently with the butter over a bain-marie, then set aside to cool a little.

2   Whisk the egg yolks and 75 g of the castor sugar in a bowl until light and frothy. Whip the egg whites in another bowl until stiff peaks form, then, while still beating, slowly add the remaining sugar.

3   Stir the melted chocolate mixture into the egg yolk mixture, along with the flour, then gently fold in the stiff egg whites. Pour the cake batter into the prepared tin, then cover the exposed surface with baking paper to prevent a crust forming during cooking.

4   Bake over a water bath for 20 minutes or until the centre is set. Test by inserting a skewer into the centre – if it comes out clean, the cake is cooked. Remove from the oven and put the tin on a wire rack to cool.

5   Peel off the top layer of baking paper and turn the cooled cake out onto the wire rack. Remove any paper still attached to the cake. When the cake has cooled completely, wrap it carefully in plastic film and store at room temperature until ready to use.

# PRALINE

## HAZELNUT PRALINE

I have used hazelnuts in this recipe but you could use almonds or pistachio nuts for a different flavour – just remember to use almond oil in this case, rather than hazelnut.

50 ml water
300 g castor sugar
hazelnut oil
250 g hazelnuts, roasted and
    skinned

1 Boil the water and castor sugar in a saucepan over a high heat without stirring until a pale caramel colour.

2 Oil a bench or marble slab with hazelnut oil and sit the roasted nuts on it. Pour the hot caramel over the nuts and let it cool completely.

3 Scrape the toffee-coated nuts off the bench with a metal spatula. Keep the chunks of praline stored in an airtight container in the refrigerator.

4 When you need some praline, process a small amount at a time in a food processor or pound it in a mortar and pestle until it forms a fine crumb.

# ARCHITECTURAL OFFERINGS

My desserts are translated as architectural offerings on the plate: visual appeal and fantasy complement texture and taste. Many of my ideas are drawn from the architecture and design that surround us in our everyday lives – I find it a challenge to transform an idea into a tangible and edible art piece without compromising that most vital component, taste.

This chapter reveals how some of these extraordinary desserts are created. It asks that you familiarise yourself with the basic techniques and methods used and gives an insight into and understanding of what motivates my work. With time, patience, reading, practice and confidence you will be able to create these desserts for yourself.

Like any other form of cooking, organisation is the key to successful dessert-making. A dish may require several steps or components, but often these can be undertaken ahead of time, leaving only the assembly. My advice is that these recipes should not be attempted at the last minute, as stress and dessert-making do not sit comfortably with each other.

Having travelled far and wide and eaten desserts in many, many establishments of varying calibre, I still believe that one of the most inspired and original creators of modern Western desserts is Phillip Searle, with whom I worked at Oasis Seros, his famed Sydney restaurant. He has an intrinsic understanding of alchemy, taste and texture, as well as the ability to push preconceived notions and practices to their limit. That experience instilled in me the value of craft, meticulous attention to detail, discipline and lateral thinking. I have adopted those practices and principles completely and can only encourage you to do the same.

# BLACKBERRIES WITH LEMON CREAM AND SHORTBREAD BISCUITS

18 Lemon Shortbread Biscuits
   (see page 19)
500 g ripe blackberries
icing sugar
6 tablespoons lemon syrup (see
   Citrus Syrup page 8)

**LEMON CREAM**
250 ml thick (45 per cent) cream
minced zest of 2 lemons
6 large egg yolks
100 g castor sugar
125 ml strained fresh lemon juice
1 gelatine leaf

I love the visual feast this dessert offers – with its components stacked on top of each other in a symmetrical tower – and its equally enticing taste. It sits there begging to be attacked! This dessert should be made when blackberries are at their peak in late summer so that they are shown to their best advantage.

1   Make the shortbread biscuits as instructed, using a 9 cm fluted pastry cutter.

2   To make the lemon cream, bring the cream and lemon zest to simmering point in a saucepan. Whisk the egg yolks and castor sugar in a bowl, then whisk in the lemon juice. Pour the warm cream into the egg mixture, stirring constantly.

3   Stand the bowl over a bain-marie and cook, stirring, until the mixture reaches the consistency of thick custard. Soften the gelatine leaf in a little cold water, then wring out the excess water and stir the gelatine into the lemon cream until dissolved. Pass the cream through a fine-meshed sieve into a clean bowl, then press a piece of plastic film down onto the surface to prevent a skin forming and refrigerate for 4 hours until cool and set.

4   To assemble the dessert, put a shortbread biscuit into the centre of each serving plate, then spoon on 1 tablespoon lemon cream. Set some blackberries, side by side, into the cream to make a circle that follows the shape of the biscuit. Put another biscuit on top of the berries, then spoon on more lemon cream. Repeat the process with the blackberries, then dust the third biscuit with icing sugar before placing it on the berries. Drizzle 1 tablespoon lemon syrup onto each plate around the biscuit stack and serve immediately.

BLACKBERRIES WITH LEMON CREAM AND SHORTBREAD BISCUITS

SAFFRON-POACHED PEARS STUFFED WITH ORANGE CARDAMOM ICE-CREAM

# SAFFRON-POACHED PEARS STUFFED WITH ORANGE CARDAMOM ICE-CREAM

The enticing aromas of this dessert make me think of the Middle East and North Africa, where these flavours are commonly used together in sweetmeat preparations. The ice-cream is my interpretation and adaptation of a well-known and loved recipe from *Jane Grigson's Fruit Book* (Stephanie Alexander also gives her version in two of her books). Credit for the idea of poaching pears in a saffron bath goes to Marieke Brugman of Howqua Dale Gourmet Retreat in Victoria, where I first came across the idea. This dessert really captures the essence of cooking with sugar and spice.

1 litre Sugar Syrup (see page 8)
375 ml sauternes
3 whole mace
zest of 2 oranges
50 ml orange-flower water
50 ml Poire William liqueur
1 teaspoon saffron threads
1 vanilla bean, split
9 ripe william *or* josephine pears

### ORANGE CARDAMOM ICE-CREAM

500 ml strained fresh orange
    juice
400 ml Sugar Syrup (see page 8)
zest of 2 oranges
5 large eggs
seeds from 4 green cardamom
    pods, ground
50 ml orange-flower water
500 ml pouring (35 per cent)
    cream

1   To make the orange cardamom ice-cream, reduce the orange juice in a stainless steel saucepan over a low heat until halved in volume (you need 250 ml). Bring the sugar syrup to simmering point with the orange zest in another saucepan, then remove the pan from the heat and strain out the zest. Whisk the eggs until light and fluffy in an electric mixer, then slowly pour in the hot sugar syrup, still beating. Whisk in the reduced orange juice, ground cardamom seeds and orange-flower water. Allow to cool, then whisk in the cream. Churn in an ice-cream machine according to the manufacturer's instructions and freeze until ready to use.

2   To prepare the pears, put the sugar syrup, sauternes, mace, orange zest, orange-flower water, Poire William and saffron threads into a wide-based saucepan and scrape in the seeds from the vanilla bean. Bring the pan to a boil, then reduce to a simmer and cook over a low heat for 15 minutes.

3   Peel, halve and core the pears and add them to the cooking liquid. Press a sheet of baking paper down onto the pears to keep them submerged to ensure even cooking and avoid discoloration. Poach the pears for 20 minutes or until soft. Remove the pears gently from the pan and set aside. Reduce the saffron liquid until it begins to thicken. Remove the pan from the heat and pass the reduced liquid through a fine-meshed sieve, then pour it over the pears and leave at room temperature until ready to serve.

4   To serve, sit 3 pear halves on each plate, then fill the cavities with little scoops of orange cardamom ice-cream. Spoon some saffron syrup over the fruit and serve immediately.

# CARAMELISED PASSIONFRUIT CREAMS WITH STRAWBERRIES AND TOFFEE WAFERS

300 g castor sugar

50 ml water

6 teaspoons Brandy Snap Biscuit
  mixture (see page 19)

18 perfect strawberries

6 tablespoons Passionfruit Syrup
  (see page 9)

**PASSIONFRUIT CREAMS**

350 ml pouring (35 per cent)
  cream

50 ml sauternes

150 ml Passionfruit Juice (see
  page 10)

2 eggs

6 large egg yolks

75 g castor sugar

Like some of the other baked creams in this chapter, this dessert is a rich and more elegant version of the universal crème caramel. This particular dessert cream takes its lead from the legendary caramelised sauternes cream invented by Phillip Searle at Oasis Seros in the late 1980s and much copied by restaurants and food writers everywhere. My love of passionfruit led me to experiment with his original concept, using the juice to give a sharp, sweet edge to the rich cream. Credit is also due to Phillip for the idea of the wafer, his version being called a 'glass' biscuit.

I use a special mould to give the wafers a corrugated appearance – the result is difficult to achieve without the mould, so I suggest you keep the wafers flat for ease of making and peace of mind.

1   Preheat the oven to 150°C. Make a caramel by boiling the castor sugar and water over a high heat without stirring. Pour the hot caramel into 6 x 150 ml dariole moulds, working quickly as the caramel will continue to cook and will darken. Tilt the moulds to ensure each is evenly lined with caramel, then discard any excess and allow to cool.

2   To make the passionfruit creams, put the cream into one stainless steel saucepan and the sauternes and passionfruit juice into another and bring both to simmering point. Gently whisk the eggs, egg yolks and castor sugar in a bowl until just amalgamated. Slowly pour the hot cream into the egg mixture, stirring constantly. Add the hot sauternes and passionfruit juice in the same way. Pass the cream mixture through a fine-meshed sieve into a jug, then pour the cream into the prepared moulds until full. Remove any surface bubbles using a teaspoon.

3   Bake the moulds in a water bath for 45 minutes or until just set. Remove the water bath from the oven and let the cooked creams sit in it until cooled. Stand the creams

on a tray, then cover them with plastic film and refrigerate for 5 hours to set before serving.

4   To make the toffee wafers, preheat the oven to 180°C. Put a teaspoonful of the brandy snap biscuit mixture on a baking tray lined with baking paper and bake for 6 minutes or until toffee-coloured. Remove the tray from the oven, then cover the biscuit with another sheet of baking paper and press gently with a flat-bottomed glass to flatten it. Allow the wafer to cool, then remove both layers of paper. Continue to make a wafer at a time until you have made 6 wafers. Store the cooled wafers in a sealed container between layers of paper to prevent them sticking and use within the day.

5   To serve, suspend each cream in hot water for 30 seconds and then carefully turn out onto a serving plate, letting the caramel pour over the cream. Slice the strawberries in half lengthwise and sit 6 halves around the base of each cream. Spoon some passionfruit syrup over the strawberries, then top with a toffee wafer and serve.

CARAMELISED PASSIONFRUIT CREAM WITH STRAWBERRIES AND TOFFEE WAFER

CANDIED CUMQUAT SPONGE PUDDING WITH ORANGE CUSTARD

# CANDIED CUMQUAT SPONGE PUDDINGS WITH ORANGE CUSTARD

Make the cumquat marmalade when the fruit is in season and you'll have an instant taste sensation on hand to make a quick and easy, comforting pudding like this one.

1   Preheat the oven to 180°C and butter and sugar 6 x 200 ml pudding moulds. To make the sponge puddings, beat the egg yolks and castor sugar in the bowl of an electric mixer until light and fluffy. With the beaters on medium speed, add the melted butter, Cointreau, orange-flower water and milk, then gently stir in the flour and baking powder.

2   Whisk the egg whites until stiff peaks form, then fold into the pudding batter. Spoon 1 tablespoon cumquat marmalade into each of the prepared moulds and pour in the batter to three-quarters fill each one. Stand the moulds in a water bath and cover the whole water bath with foil. Cook the puddings for 30 minutes, rotating the moulds at 15 minutes to ensure even cooking, then remove them from the water bath and allow to sit for 4–5 minutes before serving.

3   Make the orange custard while the puddings are cooking. Bring the cream, milk and orange zest to simmering point in a saucepan over a low heat. Whisk the egg yolks and castor sugar in a bowl until pale and frothy, then whisk in the orange juice, Cointreau and orange-flower water. Pass the hot cream mixture through a fine-meshed sieve and discard the zest, then whisk the hot cream into the egg mixture. Stand the bowl over a bain-marie and cook, whisking, until the mixture reaches a light and fluffy consistency.

4   To serve, warm the cumquat marmalade gently. Turn the puddings out of their moulds onto serving plates, using a paring knife to loosen the edges. Top with the warmed cumquat marmalade and a drizzle of orange syrup and serve with the hot orange custard.

3 teaspoons Cumquat Marmalade (see page 14)
6 teaspoons orange syrup (see Citrus Syrup page 8)

### SPONGE PUDDINGS

3 large eggs, separated
100 g castor sugar
20 g butter, melted
2 teaspoons Cointreau
1 teaspoon orange-flower water
160 ml milk
200 g self-raising flour, sifted
1 teaspoon baking powder
6 tablespoons Cumquat Marmalade (see page 14)

### ORANGE CUSTARD

250 ml pouring (35 per cent) cream
50 ml milk
zest of 2 oranges
4 egg yolks
75 g castor sugar
75 ml strained fresh orange juice
3 teaspoons Cointreau
3 teaspoons orange-flower water

# PEAR AND LIME CHARLOTTES WITH LIME CIGAR BISCUITS

6 tablespoons lime syrup (see Citrus Syrup page 8)

**LIME CIGAR BISCUITS**
50 g castor sugar
50 g unsalted butter, softened
2 egg whites
25 ml strained fresh lime juice
minced zest of 1 lime
60 g plain flour

**POACHED PEARS**
600 ml Sugar Syrup (see page 8)
100 ml sauternes
75 ml strained fresh lime juice
zest of 3 limes
½ vanilla bean
3 beurre bosc pears

**LIME JELLY**
60 ml strained fresh lime juice
60 ml Sugar Syrup (see page 8)
1 gelatine leaf

**LIME BAVAROIS**
125 ml milk
zest of 2 limes
4 egg yolks
150 g castor sugar
100 ml strained fresh lime juice
1½ gelatine leaves
250 ml thick (45 per cent) cream, whipped

Instead of the sponge of a classic charlotte, I have used poached pear here to give an interesting twist. The taste is ethereal and the dessert is as light as a feather in the mouth.

**1** To make the lime cigar biscuits, put the castor sugar and butter into the bowl of an electric mixer and beat on medium speed until white and creamy, about 10 minutes. Gradually add the egg whites to the creamed mixture, then incorporate the lime juice and zest. Add the flour and work until the dough just comes together. Spread the mixture evenly onto a buttered and floured baking tray and refrigerate for 1 hour.

**2** Preheat the oven to 140°C. Bake the biscuit sheet for 5 minutes or until golden. Remove the tray from the oven, then cut the biscuit sheet into 10 cm squares with a sharp knife. Roll each square into a cigar shape, working quickly on the hot tray as the biscuits will begin to set and become less flexible. Allow the cigars to cool on a wire rack, then store in an airtight container until ready to use.

**3** To prepare the pears, put the sugar syrup, sauternes, lime juice and zest into a wide-based saucepan and scrape in the seeds from the vanilla bean. Bring the pan to a boil, then reduce to a simmer and cook over a low heat for 10 minutes. Peel, halve and core the pears and add them to the poaching liquid. Press a sheet of baking paper down onto the pears to keep them submerged to ensure even cooking and avoid discoloration. Poach the pears for 20 minutes or until soft, then carefully remove them from the pan and set aside to cool. Reserve the poaching liquid for later use (it can be kept, refrigerated, for up to 2 months).

**4** To prepare the lime jelly, bring the lime juice and sugar syrup to a boil in a small saucepan. Soften the gelatine leaf in a little cold water, then squeeze out the excess water and stir the gelatine into the hot liquid until dissolved. Pass the hot jelly through a fine-meshed sieve into a bowl and allow to cool but not set. Spoon the cooled lime jelly into 6 x 120 ml dariole moulds – the jelly layer will be about 3 mm thick – and refrigerate until set, about 45 minutes.

**5** To make the lime bavarois, bring the milk to simmering point in a saucepan with the lime zest. Whisk the egg yolks and castor sugar in a bowl until pale and creamy, then add the lime juice and whisk in the warm milk. Stand the bowl over a bain-marie and cook, stirring, until the mixture coats the back of a spoon.

**6** Soften the gelatine leaves in a little cold water, then wring out the excess water and stir the gelatine into the custard until dissolved. Strain the custard through a fine-meshed sieve into a bowl and cool over ice in the refrigerator. When almost set (about 1 hour), whisk in the whipped cream. Refrigerate the bavarois until ready to use – don't leave it too long or it will set.

**7** To assemble the charlottes, slice the pears finely lengthwise, then line the sides of each mould with the pear, leaving a gap between each slice and making sure that the pear strips overhang the moulds. Fill each mould with the lime bavarois, then fold the pear strips over the base of each charlotte to secure. Cover with plastic film to secure and refrigerate until set, about 1 hour.

**8** To serve, suspend each charlotte in hot water for 30 seconds, then turn out onto a serving plate. Spoon the lime syrup around each charlotte and add a cigar biscuit.

PEAR AND LIME CHARLOTTE WITH LIME CIGAR BISCUIT

SOFT MERINGUE WITH MUSCAT-POACHED FRUIT AND VANILLA MASCARPONE

# SOFT MERINGUE WITH MUSCAT-POACHED FRUIT AND VANILLA MASCARPONE

**I** To make the muscat syrup, reduce the sugar syrup and liqueur muscat by half over a moderate heat in a saucepan until the consistency of syrup (you need 300 ml). Remove the pan from the heat and allow to cool completely.

**2** Preheat the oven to 160°C. Line a 4 cm deep 32 cm x 24 cm cake tin with baking paper, then lightly grease the paper with hazelnut oil.

**3** To make the soft meringue, whisk the egg whites until stiff peaks form, then gradually add the castor sugar, still beating, until thick and glossy. Fold in the vanilla essence, white vinegar and cornflour. Spread the meringue into the prepared tin with a spatula and bake for 20 minutes.

**4** Allow the meringue to cool in the tin for a few minutes after removing it from the oven. Turn the meringue out onto a sheet of baking paper that has been dusted with icing sugar and allow to cool for 10 minutes.

**5** Spread the vanilla mascarpone over the meringue and add half the muscat-poached fruit. Roll up carefully into a roulade using the paper to keep a firm shape. Cover with plastic film and refrigerate on a tray for 3 hours before serving.

**6** To serve, slice the meringue into portions and top each with some of the remaining muscat fruit, then drizzle with muscat syrup and dust with icing sugar.

hazelnut oil
sifted icing sugar
5 tablespoons Vanilla Mascarpone (see page 16)
500 g Muscat-poached Fruit (see page 13)

**MUSCAT SYRUP**
400 ml Sugar Syrup (see page 8)
200 ml liqueur muscat

**SOFT MERINGUE**
250 g egg whites
375 g castor sugar
2 teaspoons vanilla essence
2 teaspoons white vinegar
2 teaspoons cornflour

# CHOCOLATE MOCHA TART WITH ESPRESSO ICE-CREAM CONES

1 quantity Chocolate Pastry (see page 24)
525 ml pouring (35 per cent) cream
375 g dark couverture chocolate
30 ml Trablit coffee essence
340 g milk couverture chocolate
3 tablespoons Chocolate Cream (see page 17)

**ESPRESSO ICE-CREAM**
250 ml milk
100 ml strong espresso coffee
25 ml Trablit coffee essence
500 ml pouring (35 per cent) cream
6 large egg yolks
200 g castor sugar

**T**his dessert remained a constant on the Paramount menu – the demand for it seemed never-ending – and its concept and presentation of geometric precision have travelled far and wide. As I wrote in *Paramount Cooking*, this is the full-on hit for the chocolate addict.

1  To make the chocolate mocha tart, prepare and bake the tart shell as instructed.

2  To make the filling, bring 275 ml of the cream to simmering point in a saucepan. Shave the dark chocolate into a bowl and stir in the hot cream until combined, then pour into the freshly baked tart shell without delay. Refrigerate immediately and allow to set on an even surface for at least 4 hours.

3  Bring the remaining 250 ml cream to simmering point with the coffee essence. Shave the milk chocolate into a bowl and stir in the hot coffee and cream mixture until smooth. Remove the tart from the refrigerator and pour the mocha mixture over the dark chocolate layer, filling the tart right to the top of the pastry. Return the tart to the refrigerator to set firmly, about 3 hours. After the tart has set, cover with plastic film until ready to use.

4  To make the espresso ice-cream, line the inside of 6 x 12 cm high and 4 cm wide metal pastry horn moulds with baking paper. Bring the milk, espresso coffee, coffee essence and 250 ml of the cream to simmering point in a saucepan. Whisk the egg yolks and castor

sugar in a large bowl until pale and creamy, then pour in the hot cream mixture, whisking continuously. Stand the bowl over a bain-marie and cook, stirring, until the mixture coats the back of a spoon. Pass the custard through a fine-meshed sieve into a bowl, then press a piece of plastic film down onto the surface to prevent a skin forming and allow to cool.

5  Stir the remaining 250 ml cream into the cooled custard and churn in an ice-cream machine according to the manufacturer's instructions until the ice-cream is just firm enough to hold its shape. Fill a piping bag with ice-cream and pipe it into the lined moulds until almost full. Shake the moulds gently to ensure there are no air bubbles. Freeze for 4 hours or until very firm, then spoon some warm chocolate cream over the surface to form a base. Allow the cones to freeze for a further 8 hours before serving.

6  To serve the dessert, cut the chocolate mocha tart with a hot, sharp knife. Position each slice of tart across the plate. Unmould the ice-cream cones and remove the baking paper, then stand each cone on its chocolate base next to the tart.

CHOCOLATE MOCHA TART WITH ESPRESSO ICE-CREAM CONE

SUMMER PEACH AND RASPBERRY TRIFLE WITH SAUTERNES JELLY

# SUMMER PEACH AND RASPBERRY TRIFLES WITH SAUTERNES JELLY

This is a play on the famous English dessert. I've given it a refined and sophisticated touch and a sensuous, moulded appearance that lifts it out of the ordinary. You'll find you have leftover génoise – just freeze it for another day.

1  Make the génoise sponge as instructed and turn it out onto a wire rack to cool.

2  To make the sauternes jelly, bring the sauternes to simmering point in a saucepan. Soften the gelatine leaves in a little cold water, then wring out the excess water and stir the gelatine into the hot sauternes until dissolved. Pass the hot jelly through a fine-meshed sieve or muslin into a jug, then divide it equally between 6 x 9 cm wide 150 ml dome-shaped dariole moulds. Put the moulds on a tray and then allow the jelly to set in the refrigerator. This will take about 45 minutes.

3  To make the sauternes bavarois, put the milk and sauternes in separate stainless steel saucepans and bring to simmering point. Whisk the egg yolks and castor sugar in a bowl until pale and creamy, then gently whisk in the hot milk first and then the hot sauternes. Stand the bowl over a bain-marie and continue to whisk over a moderate heat until the mixture coats the back of a spoon.

4  Soften the gelatine leaves in a little cold water, then wring out the excess water and stir the gelatine into the custard until dissolved. Pass the custard through a fine-meshed sieve into another bowl, then stand this over ice to cool quickly, whisking occasionally until the custard begins to set. When the custard is cool, whip the cream until it is thick and holds its own body, then fold it evenly into the custard. Set the bavarois aside.

5  To assemble the trifles, set 9 raspberries onto the jelly layer of each mould with the pointed ends facing into the jelly. Spoon the partially set bavarois over the raspberries to cover them. At this stage the moulds should be half-full. Allow the bavarois layer to set completely in the refrigerator – this will take about 1 hour.

6  When the bavarois has set, peel the peaches, then cut them into eighths. Carefully arrange the peach slices evenly over the bavarois layer, ensuring the thicker edges face the outside of the moulds (this will help keep the trifles stable when they are turned out).

7  Cut 6 x 1 cm thick rounds from the sponge the same diameter as the moulds. Brush each piece of sponge with some of the liquid in which the peaches were preserved, then put these carefully on top of the peaches. The cake should lie flat with the top of the mould so that when turned out it will sit evenly on the plate. Wrap each mould with plastic film, twisting the ends together underneath to secure it tightly. Allow the trifles to set in the refrigerator for at least 3 hours before turning out.

8  To serve the trifles, smear the centre of each serving plate with 25 ml of the raspberry sauce. Fill a wide bowl with very hot water. Unwrap the moulds and invert them, one at a time, into the hot water for 10–20 seconds. Turn each mould upside down and let the trifle slide out onto your hand, then carefully place it on the sauce puddle and serve immediately.

1 Génoise Sponge (see page 27)
250 g perfect raspberries
6 Brandied Peaches
    (see page 12)
150 ml Raspberry Sauce
    (see page 10)

**SAUTERNES JELLY**
210 ml sauternes
1½ gelatine leaves

**SAUTERNES BAVAROIS**
100 ml full-cream milk
100 ml sauternes
4 large egg yolks
90 g castor sugar
1½ gelatine leaves
225 ml thick (45 per cent) cream

# RASPBERRY AND YARRA VALLEY CLOTTED CREAM TARTS

1 quantity Sweet Pastry (see
   page 22)
750 g raspberries
300 g Yarra Valley Dairy clotted
   cream
100 g icing sugar

**T**hese tarts are extremely simple to make and are a special salute to the fantastic clotted cream being made in Australia, especially by Richard Thomas at the Yarra Valley Dairy in Victoria. A celebration of stylish simplicity.

**1**   Prepare the pastry and blind bake 6 small tart shells as instructed.

**2**   Mash 250 g of the raspberries with the clotted cream and the 100 g icing sugar in a bowl to create a raspberry ripple effect.

**3**   Spoon the cream mixture evenly into each tart shell, then arrange the remaining raspberries on the cream with their pointed ends facing up and dust with a little extra icing sugar before serving.

# APRICOTS AND CARDAMOM CREAM
# WITH MERINGUES

This dessert is another version of the 'stack' idea, each layer offering a different texture. Cardamom lends itself extremely well to dessert work and is a natural accompaniment to apricots. Here it adds a gentle and interesting spiciness that cuts through the richness of the cream.

1 quantity Meringue mixture
(see page 15)
6 teaspoons crushed Praline (see
page 29)

**POACHED APRICOTS**
1 litre Sugar Syrup (see page 8)
10 green cardamom pods,
cracked open
1 vanilla bean, split
250 ml sauternes
125 ml brandy
18 apricots

**CARDAMOM CREAM**
400 ml thick (45 per cent) cream
12 green cardamom pods,
cracked open
6 large egg yolks
50 g castor sugar
½ gelatine leaf
½ teaspoon freshly ground
cardamom seeds

1   Preheat the oven to 50°C and line a baking tray with baking paper. Make the meringue mixture as instructed, then spoon it into a piping bag fitted with a 5 mm plain round nozzle. Pipe the meringue onto the baking tray to make 12 x 8 cm discs (you may want to draw circles onto the paper first). Cook the meringues for 45 minutes until firm but not coloured. Allow the meringues to cool on a wire rack before storing them in an airtight container until ready to use.

2   To prepare the apricots, bring all the ingredients except the apricots to a boil in a wide-based saucepan. Add the apricots to the syrup, then simmer gently for 20 minutes until the fruit has softened. Remove the fruit from the syrup using a slotted spoon and allow it to cool a little. Cut the apricots in half and remove the stones, then set aside.

3   Return the poaching liquid to the stove, then add the apricot stones and cook over a high heat until more syrupy. Pass the syrup through a fine-meshed sieve into a bowl, discarding the solids, and allow to cool.

4   To make the cardamom cream, bring the cream and cardamom pods to simmering point in a saucepan over a low heat. Whisk the egg yolks and castor sugar in a bowl, then whisk in the hot cream mixture. Stand the bowl over a bain-marie and cook, stirring, until the mixture reaches the consistency of thick custard. Soften the gelatine leaf in a little cold water, then wring out the excess water and stir the gelatine into the custard until dissolved. Pass the mixture through a fine-meshed sieve into a bowl, then stir in the ground cardamom seeds. Press plastic film down onto the surface of the cream to prevent a skin forming and stand the bowl over ice in the refrigerator until set, about 4 hours.

5   To assemble, place 1 meringue on each serving plate. Slice the apricots and arrange some over each meringue. Spoon cardamom cream over the fruit, then add more sliced apricot. Drizzle some of the reserved poaching syrup over the fruit and top each stack with another meringue. Sprinkle praline over each dessert and serve immediately.

# VANILLA MASCARPONE CREAM HEARTS WITH RASPBERRIES AND BLACKBERRIES

150 g Vanilla Mascarpone (see page 16)
100 g cream cheese
125 g castor sugar
250 ml thick (45 per cent) cream
125 g thick plain yoghurt
250 g fresh raspberries
250 g fresh blackberries
6 tablespoons Raspberry Sauce (see page 10)

This is one of the serious classics of French cooking and uses a soft white cheese as its base. My version combines mascarpone and yoghurt to give a more complex, sharp and interesting flavour that works in heady harmony with red summer berries. The cream is formed in traditional heart-shaped porcelain moulds that have holes in the base to allow whey to drain away, giving the cream a firmer texture. After the cream has been refrigerated for several hours, it is unmoulded to reveal its perfect form.

Other red berries, such as redcurrants, strawberries, boysenberries or youngberries, can also be used when they are in season. I have also served this cream heart successfully with Poached Quinces (see page 11) and some of their perfumed syrup.

1   Chill the bowl and blade of a food processor in the refrigerator.

2   To make the cream hearts, blend the mascarpone, cream cheese and castor sugar in the food processor until smooth. Scrape the sides of the bowl with a plastic spatula occasionally to keep the mixture evenly distributed. Add the cream and yoghurt and blend briefly to incorporate.

3   Line 6 porcelain heart moulds with a double layer of wet muslin and carefully spoon in the cream mixture until the moulds are full and the surface is even. Put the moulds on a tray with a lip (to catch the whey), then cover with plastic film and refrigerate for at least 8 hours before serving.

4   To serve, arrange the raspberries and blackberries in the centre of each serving plate and spoon the raspberry sauce over the berries. Lift the cream hearts out of their moulds using the muslin, then invert each heart onto the berries and carefully remove the muslin. Serve immediately.

VANILLA MASCARPONE CREAM HEART WITH RASPBERRIES AND BLACKBERRIES

PASSIONFRUIT FLOATING ISLANDS

# PASSIONFRUIT FLOATING ISLANDS

This dessert is a tribute to the wonders of passionfruit, this time playing on the classic French dessert *île flottante*, also known as *oeufs à la neige* or snow eggs. A very easy dessert to prepare and a great light finish to a meal.

1  Make the meringue mixture as instructed. Bring the milk to simmering point in a wide-based saucepan. Shape the meringue into quenelles with a spoon dipped in hot water, then gently poach a few at a time in the milk until cooked and holding their shape, about 5 minutes (turn the quenelles halfway through cooking). Set aside while making the passionfruit custard – the meringues can be made up to 2 hours ahead.

2  To make the passionfruit custard, put the cream and the passionfruit juice in separate saucepans and bring each to simmering point. Whisk the egg yolks and castor sugar in a bowl until light and fluffy. Pour the warm cream into the egg mixture in a thin, slow stream, whisking gently. Repeat the process with the passionfruit juice. Stand the bowl over a bain-marie and cook, whisking continuously, until the mixture coats the back

of a spoon. Pass the custard through a fine-meshed sieve into a bowl, then press a piece of plastic film down onto the surface to prevent a skin forming and set aside until ready to use.

3  Just before serving, make a toffee by boiling the castor sugar and water in a saucepan over a high heat without stirring until caramel-coloured. Allow to cool a little.

4  To serve, pour the hot passionfruit custard into serving bowls (reheat the custard gently over a bain-marie, whisking continuously, if you have made it ahead). Float 2 meringues in each bowl of custard, then spoon the pulp from the passionfruit over them. Using a spoon, drizzle fine threads of toffee over the meringues. (The toffee becomes easier to use as it is cools, when it starts to hold its shape.) Serve immediately.

1 quantity Meringue mixture
  (see page 15)
500 ml milk
200 g castor sugar
50 ml water
6 passionfruit

**PASSIONFRUIT CUSTARD**
500 ml pouring (35 per cent)
  cream
250 ml Passionfruit Juice (see
  page 10)
8 egg yolks
150 g castor sugar

# MISSION FIGS AND MILAWA BLUE GOAT'S CHEESE BAKED IN PASTRY WITH MUSCAT FIG GLAZE

1 quantity Puff Pastry (see page 20)
75 g seedless muscatels
125 ml liqueur muscat
250 g ripe mission figs, chopped
125 g Milawa Mt Buffalo Blue cheese, crumbled
1 egg yolk, lightly beaten

**MUSCAT FIG GLAZE**
200 ml liqueur muscat
500 ml Sugar Syrup (see page 8)
12 mission figs, chopped

These little pies are a play on the classic French pithiviers and can be served in place of a cheese course during dinner or as a finale to a lunch menu. They are made purposely small because they are rich. The glaze can be served separately in a jug to be added at the whim of the eater.

Mission figs are a small black variety available in autumn. While I like to use the Milawa Cheese Company's Mt Buffalo Blue, a goat's cheese, for this dish, any other blue cheese can be substituted. Roquefort is good too.

1   Prepare and chill the puff pastry as instructed.

2   Soak the muscatels in the liqueur muscat for 1 hour.

3   To make the pastries, roll out the puff pastry on a floured surface until 1 cm thick. Using pastry cutters, cut out 6 × 10 cm lids and 6 × 8 cm bases. Refrigerate the pastry rounds until required.

4   To make the filling, strain the liqueur from the muscatels and reserve it for use in the glaze. Gently combine the muscatels, chopped figs and crumbled cheese in a bowl with your hands, then form the mixture into 6 balls. Brush the pastry bases with the egg yolk and place a ball of filling on each base. Cover with the pastry lids, then press the edges together with your fingers and smooth them with a paring knife. Brush the lids with egg yolk and score 6 arcs around the dome of each, working from the top down. Refrigerate the pastries for 1 hour before baking.

5   To make the muscat fig glaze, bring all the ingredients to a boil in a saucepan, including the reserved liqueur, and simmer for 30 minutes over a low heat until reduced. Pass the syrup through a fine-meshed sieve, discarding the solids.

6   Preheat the oven to 180°C. Bake the pastries for 10 minutes until golden, then serve with the muscat fig glaze while hot.

MISSION FIGS AND MILAWA BLUE GOAT'S CHEESE BAKED IN PASTRY WITH MUSCAT FIG GLAZE

CHOCOLATE JAFFA MOUSSE CAKE WITH ORANGE CARAMEL

# CHOCOLATE JAFFA MOUSSE CAKE WITH ORANGE CARAMEL

The starting point for this cake was the heady combination of dark chocolate and orange first experienced in the Jaffas of our youth, eaten ferociously at the movies and often rolled down the aisles. Jaffa, in fact, is a coastal town near Tel Aviv in Israel where the orange is first thought to have been cultivated. Today the town gives its name to the oranges and pink grapefruit grown and marketed there.

1   Preheat the oven to 160°C and grease and line a 32 cm x 24 cm cake tin. Make the doubled chocolate fudge cake mixture as instructed, adding the minced orange zest to the egg mixture before folding in the egg whites. Pour the cake mixture into the tin, then cover the exposed surface with baking paper to prevent a crust forming during cooking. Bake over a water bath for 20 minutes or until the centre has set. Test by inserting a skewer into the centre – if it comes out clean, the cake is cooked. Remove from the oven and put the tin on a wire rack to cool.

2   Peel off the top layer of baking paper and turn the cooled cake out onto the wire rack. Remove any paper still attached to the cake. When the cake has cooled completely, wrap it carefully in plastic film and refrigerate until ready to use.

3   To make the chocolate jaffa mousse, bring the milk and orange zest to simmering point in a saucepan. Whisk the egg yolks and castor sugar in a bowl until pale and creamy, then whisk in the orange juice. Whisk the hot milk into the egg mixture.

4   Melt the chocolate gently in a bowl over a bain-marie. Meanwhile, soften the gelatine leaves in a little cold water, then wring out the excess water and stir the gelatine into the egg mixture until dissolved. Stand the bowl over another bain-marie and cook until the mixture

coats the back of a spoon. Pass the custard through a fine-meshed sieve into a bowl and discard the orange zest. Stir the melted chocolate into the custard, then stir over ice until cool. Fold the whipped cream into the custard and set aside but not for more than 30 minutes or it will set.

5   To make the orange caramel, boil the castor sugar and water in a saucepan over a high heat without stirring until caramel-coloured. Reduce the heat, then add the orange juice and zest and cook for a further 10 minutes until the juice has worked into the caramel. Remove the pan from the heat, then pour the orange caramel into a jug and allow to cool at room temperature.

6   To assemble the dessert, line a 32 cm x 8 cm x 8 cm mould with baking paper, leaving a little extending past the tin (this will help you lift the cake out later on). Cut 1 cm thick slices of chocolate fudge cake and line the bottom and sides of the mould. Fill the mould with the unset chocolate mousse and then add another layer of cake to seal. Cover with plastic film and refrigerate for 5 hours to set.

7   To serve, remove the plastic and lift the cake out of its mould using the paper lining to help you. Cut the cake into 3 cm thick slices (or a wedge instead) with a hot, wet knife. Sit a slice of cake on each serving plate, then add some orange caramel and serve.

2 quantities Chocolate Fudge
   Cake mixture (see page 28)
minced zest of 1 orange

**CHOCOLATE JAFFA MOUSSE**
200 ml milk
zest of 2 oranges
4 egg yolks
100 g castor sugar
50 ml strained fresh orange juice
150 g dark couverture chocolate
2 gelatine leaves
300 ml thick (45 per cent)
   cream, whipped

**ORANGE CARAMEL**
300 g castor sugar
100 ml water
150 ml strained fresh orange
   juice
zest of 3 oranges

# MERINGUES WITH BRANDIED CHERRIES, CLOTTED CREAM AND PRALINE

1 quantity Meringue mixture
  (see page 15)
300 g clotted cream
6 tablespoons Brandied Cherries
  (see page 12), drained
1 quantity Cherry Syrup
  (see page 8)
6 teaspoons Praline
  (see page 29)

**A**s with the dessert of muscat-poached fruit with meringue in *Paramount Cooking*, I use a meringue structure here to show the rich colour of the fruit to its best advantage with a little folly. The meringue draws its inspiration from the famed Gaudi architecture of Barcelona. Like its predecessor, the sugary walls of this confection hide the fruit and cream filling from the initial glance; once the meringue is broken, all is revealed. The fabulous appearance of this structure is equalled by the texture and taste of the ensemble.

The meringues require long, slow cooking but can be prepared well ahead and stored in an airtight container. With the cherries in the pantry, this dessert can then be put together in minutes.

**1**  Preheat the oven to 50°C. Make the meringue mixture as instructed. Remember that it must be stiff so that it doesn't collapse on the moulds later on. Spoon the mixture into a piping bag fitted with a plain 1 cm round nozzle.

**2**  Line 6 × 12 cm high × 4 cm wide metal pastry horn moulds with baking paper. Fold the excess paper into the hollow centre to secure the lining. Working from the bottom up, pipe the meringue onto each mould in upward, even strokes, finishing each time with a flick of the wrist to form a spiked peak. Make sure each new meringue piping joins the next so that there are no gaps.

**3**  Put the meringue cones onto a baking tray lined with baking paper and cook for 8 hours or until firm but not coloured. Allow the meringues to cool, then carefully remove them from their moulds and store upright in an airtight container until ready to use.

**4**  To assemble the dessert, invert one meringue at a time in your hand, then spoon in some of the clotted cream, followed by brandied cherries and then more cream. Turn the meringue over quickly and sit it on its cream base on the plate. Spoon a few extra cherries on top of each meringue, then drizzle with the cherry syrup and sprinkle with 1 teaspoon praline. Serve immediately.

MERINGUE WITH BRANDIED CHERRIES, CLOTTED CREAM AND PRALINE

PASSIONFRUIT MIROIR

# PASSIONFRUIT MIROIRS

This recipe appeared in my first book, *Paramount Cooking*. It deserves prominence here because of its soft and sublime texture and its strong and clean taste. And it is a personal favourite – it is passionfruit, after all! For me, passionfruit is the ultimate fruit – and its popularity is shared by many dessert fiends.

1  Make the génoise sponge as instructed and turn it out onto a wire rack to cool.

2  To make the passionfruit bavarois, bring the milk to simmering point in a saucepan. Whisk the egg yolks and castor sugar in a bowl until pale and frothy, then add the passionfruit juice and slowly whisk in the warm milk. Stand the bowl over a bain-marie and gently cook, whisking continuously, until the mixture coats the back of a spoon.

3  Soften the gelatine leaves in a little cold water, then wring out the excess water and stir the gelatine into the custard until dissolved. Pass the custard through a fine-meshed sieve into a clean bowl and cool over ice in the refrigerator. When the custard has almost set (about 1 hour), whisk in the whipped cream. Refrigerate the bavarois until ready to use.

4  To make the passionfruit jelly, bring the passionfruit juice and sugar syrup to a boil in a saucepan. Soften the gelatine leaves in a little cold water, then wring out the excess water and stir the gelatine into the hot liquid until dissolved. Pass the hot jelly through a fine-meshed sieve into a bowl and allow to cool but not set.

5  To assemble the miroirs, spoon the cool jelly into 6 × 150 ml dariole moulds 6 cm in diameter – you should have a 3 mm thick layer. Refrigerate until set, about 45 minutes. Spoon the bavarois on top of the jelly, filling the moulds until 5 mm from the top. Refrigerate until set, about 1 hour.

6  Cut the génoise sponge into 6 rounds that are the same diameter as the moulds and 5 mm thick. Position a cake round on top of each bavarois, then cover tightly with plastic film to secure and refrigerate for 4 hours before serving.

7  To serve, suspend each miroir in hot water for 30 seconds, then carefully turn out onto a serving plate and spoon passionfruit syrup around the base of each one.

1 Génoise Sponge (see page 27)
1 quantity Passionfruit Syrup
    (see page 9)

### PASSIONFRUIT BAVAROIS

125 ml milk
4 large egg yolks
150 g castor sugar
100 ml Passionfruit Juice
    (see page 10)
2 gelatine leaves
250 ml thick (45 per cent)
    cream, stiffly whipped

### PASSIONFRUIT JELLY

90 ml Passionfruit Juice
    (see page 10)
90 ml Sugar Syrup (see page 8)
1½ gelatine leaves

# STRAWBERRY AND VANILLA CREAM SHORTCAKES

1 quantity Thick Vanilla Cream
(see page 16)
500 g ripe strawberries
6 tablespoons Strawberry Sauce
(see page 10)
icing sugar (optional)

**ALMOND CAKE**
6 large eggs, separated
250 g castor sugar
250 g ground almonds

**T**his is my version of an American classic that is based around a crumbly cake or biscuit, fruit and whipped cream. I use a nutty meringue cake that has a soft, light texture – it carries the sweetness of ripe, tropical strawberries and the richness of vanilla cream fabulously well. If you ever come across them, use the alpine strawberries grown around Orange in New South Wales. Their season is extremely short – around April and May – and supply is minimal but they are very similar to the exceptional tiny wild strawberries of southern France (*fraises des bois*) that are abundant in the European spring.

**1** Preheat the oven to 180°C and grease and line a 24 cm x 20 cm cake tin.

**2** To make the cake, whisk the egg yolks and 125 g of the castor sugar until pale and creamy, then stir in the ground almonds. In another bowl, whip the egg whites until stiff peaks form, then slowly add the remaining castor sugar, still whisking. Gently fold the egg white mixture into the almond mixture, then pour this into the prepared tin and bake for 25 minutes. Remove the cake from the oven and turn out onto a wire rack to cool. When cooled, cut into 12 x 8 cm rounds using a pastry cutter.

**3** To serve, put a round of cake on each serving plate, then top with the vanilla cream, some sliced strawberries and another round of cake. Add a dob of vanilla cream and sit a whole strawberry in it, then spoon some strawberry sauce around the cake. Dust with icing sugar, if you like, and serve.

STRAWBERRY AND VANILLA CREAM SHORTCAKE

BAKED RHUBARB AND HAZELNUT MACAROON CRUMBLE

# BAKED RHUBARB AND HAZELNUT
# MACAROON CRUMBLE

This dessert is a special tribute to my grandmother Pearl, who religiously made an apple crumble at least once a week for us during my formative years, just as she had done for her own children. It was always an instant hit! Like many grandmothers, she was an avid baker, constantly at the stove whipping up cakes, biscuits, pastries and the like, when morning tea and afternoon tea were a ritual and gave a sense of order to the day. This is a 'posh' modern interpretation of a down-home classic and is very easy to put together – just find the right beautiful dish to serve it in and it looks quite regal in its own way.

12 stalks rhubarb
100 g castor sugar
30 ml strained fresh lemon juice

**CRUMBLE**
75 g Butter Brioche crumbs (see
   page 26)
75 g hazelnut Macaroons (see
   page 141), broken
60 g unsalted butter
50 g dark-brown sugar
50 g plain flour
minced zest of 1 lemon
½ teaspoon ground cinnamon
¼ teaspoon freshly grated
   nutmeg

1   Wash the rhubarb and chop the stalks into 3 cm lengths, then put them in a stainless steel saucepan with the castor sugar and lemon juice and cook over a moderate heat until the rhubarb has softened but still holds its shape. Remove the rhubarb from the heat, then divide between 6 small gratin dishes and pour over the cooking juices.

2   Preheat an overhead griller. To make the crumble, mix all the ingredients in a bowl by hand until well incorporated and crumbly in appearance. Sprinkle the mixture over the rhubarb and brown under the griller for 5–6 minutes until the crumble cooks and softens under the heat. Serve with clotted cream, whipped cream or ice-cream.

# CARAMELISED GINGER CREAMS WITH GINGERBREAD AND GLAZED PEAR

## GINGERBREAD

175 g self-raising flour
½ teaspoon baking powder
2 teaspoons ground ginger
1 teaspoon ground cinnamon
100 g unsalted butter
70 ml golden syrup
125 g dark-brown sugar
2 large eggs, beaten
125 ml milk
50 g crème fraîche
2 teaspoons minced candied
　　ginger

## GINGER CREAMS

300 g castor sugar
50 ml water
350 ml thick (45 per cent) cream
100 ml milk
50 ml green ginger wine
2 tablespoons minced fresh
　　ginger
2 eggs
6 large egg yolks
75 g castor sugar

## POACHED PEARS

750 ml Sugar Syrup (see page 8)
1 tablespoon minced fresh ginger
150 ml green ginger wine
250 ml Poire William liqueur
6 ripe beurre bosc pears

This dessert is a celebration of the versatility and flavour of ginger, the spicy and pungent taste intensifying with each layer.

1   To make the gingerbread, preheat the oven to 160°C and grease and line a 15 cm square cake tin. Sift the flour, baking powder, ground ginger and cinnamon into a bowl.

2   Melt the butter with the golden syrup and dark-brown sugar in a saucepan over a moderate heat. Whisk the eggs with the milk, crème fraîche and candied ginger in a bowl, then add the melted syrup mixture and stir well. Stir the liquid into the sifted dry ingredients, then tip the batter into the prepared tin. Bake for 35 minutes or until cooked. Test by inserting a skewer into the centre – if it comes out clean, the cake is cooked. Remove the cake from the oven, then leave it to cool in the tin for 5 minutes before turning it out onto a wire rack.

3   To make the ginger creams, preheat the oven to 150°C. Make a caramel by boiling the castor sugar and water over a high heat without stirring. Pour the hot caramel into 6 × 150 ml dariole moulds, working quickly as the caramel will continue to cook and will darken. Tilt the moulds to ensure each is evenly lined with caramel, then discard any excess and allow the caramel to cool.

4   Bring the cream, milk, green ginger wine and fresh ginger to simmering point in a saucepan over a low heat. Whisk the eggs, egg yolks and castor sugar in a bowl until just incorporated, then gently whisk in the hot cream mixture. Pass the custard through a fine-meshed sieve into a jug, then fill the prepared moulds. Remove any surface bubbles using a teaspoon. Bake the creams in a water bath for 35 minutes – they may need another

5–10 minutes, but keep an eye on them to ensure even cooking. Don't let them colour on top as they will form an unpleasant skin. Remove the water bath from the oven and take the creams out of the water. Allow them to cool, then refrigerate for at least 5 hours before serving.

5   To poach the pears, put the sugar syrup, fresh ginger, green ginger wine and Poire William in a wide-based stainless steel saucepan and bring to a boil. Simmer for 15 minutes to intensify the flavour and reduce the liquid slightly. Peel, halve and core the pears and lie them gently in the poaching liquid. Press baking paper down onto the pears to keep them submerged to ensure even cooking and avoid discoloration, then simmer gently until cooked and softened, about 30 minutes. Remove the pears from the poaching liquid, then slice them in half again and set aside. Reduce the liquid over a medium heat until it reaches the consistency of syrup, then pass it through a fine-meshed sieve and discard the solids. Allow the syrup to cool, then pour it over the poached pear and keep cool until ready to serve.

6   To serve, cut out 3 rounds of gingerbread using a pastry cutter the same diameter as the base of the creams. Cut these rounds through the middle to make each one 2 cm thick. Sit a round of cake in the centre of each serving plate. Suspend each ginger cream in hot water for 30 seconds and then carefully turn out onto the gingerbread, letting the caramel pour over the cream. Place 4 pieces of pear around the base of each cream and spoon some of the reserved poaching syrup over the fruit.

CARAMELISED GINGER CREAM WITH GINGERBREAD AND GLAZED PEAR

RHUBARB AND CLOTTED CREAM TART

# RHUBARB AND CLOTTED CREAM TARTS

An extremely simple dessert to prepare, these tarts combine perfect pastry, fruit and fantastic clotted cream and are a taste sensation. Actually a vegetable, rhubarb is under-rated and perceived as old-fashioned, partly because the English have always done such dreadful things with it. Try this easy preparation and see if it changes your mind!

1 quantity Sweet Pastry (see
    page 22)
12 stalks rhubarb
100 g castor sugar
30 ml strained fresh lemon juice
300 g clotted cream

1   Prepare the pastry and blind bake 6 small tart shells as instructed.

2   Wash the rhubarb and cut the stalks into 3 cm lengths, then cook them with the castor sugar and lemon juice in a frying pan over a gentle heat until the rhubarb has softened but still holds its shape. Remove the pan from the heat, then strain the juice from the rhubarb and reserve. Allow the rhubarb to cool. Reduce the cooking liquid slightly over heat until a little thicker.

3   To serve, mix half the cooled rhubarb into the clotted cream and spoon into the tart shells. Arrange the remaining rhubarb on the cream, then spoon some reduced rhubarb liquid over and serve.

# LIME AND COCONUT SAGO PUDDINGS WITH RED PAPAYA AND COCONUT WAFERS

½ quantity Coconut Wafers (see
  page 135)
1 small red papaya
2 teaspoons strained fresh lime
  juice

**LIME JELLY**
125 ml strained fresh lime juice
125 ml Sugar Syrup (see page 8)
2 gelatine leaves

**SAGO PUDDINGS**
750 ml water
200 ml coconut milk
125 g coconut sugar, shaved
250 g sago
2 teaspoons minced lime zest
1 egg white

**COCONUT CREAM SAUCE**
100 g coconut sugar, shaved
75 ml water
100 ml coconut cream

This dessert looks to our neighbours in South East Asia for its flavour and texture. Sago or tapioca is a common ingredient in Asian sweetmeats. This starch has the appearance of tiny white pearls; these soften but hold their shape with cooking, having no inherent flavour but acting as a textural carrier and thickening agent.

Coconut sugar is similar to palm sugar as it comes in block form and is caramel in colour but it has an intense coconut flavour. It is available from Asian food stores.

1  Make the coconut wafers as instructed but let them cool flat rather than mould them.

2  To make the lime jelly, bring the lime juice and sugar syrup to simmering point in a saucepan. Soften the gelatine leaves in a little cold water, then wring out the excess water and stir the gelatine into the hot liquid until dissolved. Pass the hot jelly through a fine-meshed sieve, then pour it into 6 × 120 ml dariole moulds and allow to set in the refrigerator, about 1 hour.

3  To make the sago puddings, bring the water, coconut milk and coconut sugar to a boil in a saucepan. Add the sago and lime zest and cook over a moderate heat, stirring continuously, until the sago becomes transparent and the mixture is thick. Remove the pan from the heat and allow to cool slightly. Whisk the egg white until stiff, then fold it into the sago. Spoon the mixture over the lime jelly in the moulds and refrigerate, covered with plastic film, for 2 hours until set.

4  To make the coconut cream sauce, bring the coconut sugar and water to a boil in a saucepan, then strain to remove any impurities. Stir in the coconut cream, then remove from the heat immediately and allow to cool before serving.

5  To serve, halve and peel the papaya, then remove the seeds. Finely slice the papaya into 5 cm lengths, then arrange a flat stack on each serving plate and sprinkle with lime juice. To turn out the sago puddings, suspend the moulds in hot water for 30 seconds and turn out onto the papaya. Spoon some coconut cream sauce around the fruit, then lean a coconut wafer against each pudding and serve immediately.

LIME AND COCONUT SAGO PUDDING WITH RED PAPAYA AND COCONUT WAFER

# BAKED RICOTTA AND CANDIED FRUIT TARTS WITH ORANGE SYRUP

350 g ricotta

1 quantity Sweet Orange Pastry
(see page 22)

3 large eggs, separated

100g castor sugar

zest of 1 lemon

75 g butter, melted

40 g plain flour

pinch of sea salt

25 g finely diced candied citron

25 g finely diced candied orange
peel

25 g finely diced candied
grapefruit peel

25 g finely diced candied ginger

icing sugar

120 ml orange syrup (see Citrus
Syrup page 8)

**T**hese tarts are extremely easy to prepare and are a type of cheesecake with a more ethereal texture; the candied fruit adds further dimension. They are best eaten warm when they are light and airy – left to cool they tend to deflate.

Look for a fairly dry ricotta for this dish. Some fantastic Australian examples are available now: I especially like Gabrielle Kervella's goat's ricotta and Simon Burr and Paula Jenkin's Woodside Cheese Wrights goat's curd.

**1**   Stand the ricotta in a sieve lined with a double layer of muslin and allow to drain over a bowl in the refrigerator overnight.

**2**   Prepare the pastry and blind bake 6 small tart shells as instructed.

**3**   Preheat the oven to 150°C. Blend the drained ricotta with the egg yolks and castor sugar in an electric mixer until smooth.  Add the lemon zest, melted butter, flour and salt and work briefly – do not overwhip. Stir the candied fruit in by hand.  Whisk the egg whites until soft peaks form, then fold gently into the ricotta mixture.

**4**   Pour the ricotta mixture into the tart shells and bake for 20 minutes or until set. Remove the tarts from the oven and allow them to stand in their tins for 5 minutes before transferring them to serving plates. Dust each tart with icing sugar, then spoon a little orange syrup around them and serve while warm.

# PASSIONFRUIT CURD AND MANGO TARTS

Passionfruit curd is as indispensable to me as Lemon Curd (see page 15), and as it keeps well refrigerated I always have it on hand. This means I can enjoy passionfruit's intense taste of sunshine during the gloomiest times of the year! I recommend, however that you make these wonderfully simple tarts at the height of summer when both passionfruit and mangoes are at their best for a full-on tropical taste sensation.

1  Prepare the pastry and blind bake 6 small tart shells as instructed.

2  To make the passionfruit curd, whisk the egg yolks and castor sugar in a bowl until light and fluffy. Add the passionfruit juice, then stand the bowl over a bain-marie and cook until thick, stirring constantly.

3  Add the butter piece by piece, allowing each piece to incorporate before adding the next. The mixture should have become thicker by the time the last piece of butter has been added. Remove the bowl from the heat and stand it over ice to cool. Store the curd in the refrigerator until ready to use.

4  To assemble, slice the cheeks of the mangoes from the seeds, then remove the skin and finely slice the flesh lengthwise. Arrange the sliced mango across the base of each tart shell, then fill the tarts with the passionfruit curd. Cut the passionfruit in half and scoop the pulp over the curd, then drizzle passionfruit syrup around each tart and serve immediately.

1 quantity Sweet Pastry (see page 22)
2 ripe mangoes
3 passionfruit
120 ml Passionfruit Syrup (see page 9)

**PASSIONFRUIT CURD**
5 large egg yolks
100 g castor sugar
110 ml Passionfruit Juice (see page 10)
125 g unsalted butter, chilled

ORANGE AND CARDAMOM CREAM TART WITH KAKADU BREAD DATES

# ORANGE AND CARDAMOM CREAM TARTS WITH KAKADU BREAD DATES

This dessert was inspired by the flavours of the Middle East and those common in the cooking of North Africa. Fresh sweet dates from the Northern Territory are now making an appearance on the market in limited quantities when they are in season in late winter and early spring. If you can't locate them, you can substitute the more readily available fresh medjool dates from California or fresh Turkish dates. If you'd rather make one large tart than individual tarts, try a rectangular 34 cm x 10 cm tin.

1 quantity Sweet Orange Pastry (see page 22)
4 large eggs
180 g castor sugar
zest of 2 oranges
120 ml strained fresh orange juice
seeds from 4 green cardamom pods, ground
150 ml pouring (35 per cent) cream
18 fresh Kakadu bread dates, halved and stoned
icing sugar
6 tablespoons orange syrup (see Citrus Syrup page 8)

1   Prepare the pastry and blind bake 6 x 10 cm tart shells as instructed.

2   Whisk the eggs and castor sugar until light and frothy. Stir in the orange zest and juice, ground cardamom seeds and cream and refrigerate overnight.

3   Next day, preheat the oven to 160°C. Pass the egg mixture through a fine-meshed sieve and discard the solids. Stand the tart shells on a baking tray, then divide the dates between them, cut-side down, and gently pour in the egg mixture. Bake the tarts for 30 minutes or until the custard has set. Remove the tarts from the oven and allow to cool for 3 hours before removing the tins.

4   Put each tart in the centre of a serving plate, then dust with icing sugar and spoon some orange syrup around the base. (Sometimes I serve a few extra dates alongside and douse these with the orange syrup instead.)

# BAKED BLOOD PLUM BRIOCHES WITH SPICED PLUM SAUCE AND VANILLA CUSTARD

6 blood plums, halved and
   stoned
6 teaspoons castor sugar
1 quantity Cinnamon Brioche
   dough (see page 27)
200 ml Vanilla Custard (see
   page 17)
icing sugar

**SPICED PLUM SAUCE**
1 litre water
1 kg castor sugar
100 ml brandy
150 ml cassis
1 vanilla bean, split
1 stick cinnamon
3 cloves
2 whole mace
2 kg blood plums, halved and
   stoned

Blood plums, the red stone fruit of summer, have a long season and good shelf-life. They are wonderful in their natural state and also lend themselves extremely well to cooking (especially with spices) and preserving.

You only need a small amount of the sauce for this dessert, so preserve what you don't need by filling hot, sterilised jars with the just-made sauce. Use it with ice-cream, a red fruit salad or a plum tart lined with vanilla cream. In *Paramount Cooking* I suggest making spiced plums – follow the instructions below but remove the plums from the heat when cooked but still intact. These plums need to be peeled before they are used.

1   To make the spiced plum sauce, put all the ingredients except the plums into a large stainless steel stockpot and bring to a boil, then simmer for 20 minutes. Add the plums to the syrup and cook over a low heat for 1 hour or until the plums have lost their shape and become mushy.

2   Press the contents of the pot through a conical sieve, extracting as much juice as possible and discarding the solids. The sauce can be used right away or kept for later use.

3   Preheat an overhead griller. Put the plum halves, cut-side up, on a baking tray and sprinkle with the castor sugar. Grill until the fruit starts to soften and the sugar colours, then allow to cool.

4   Make the brioche dough as instructed, then butter and sugar 6 small brioche tins and preheat the oven to 200°C. After the dough has doubled in volume, punch it down and divide it into 6 pieces. Roll out each piece into a round shape on a floured surface and put 2 plum halves, reformed to make a 'whole', in the centre. Mould the brioche dough around the fruit filling to secure it and transfer to the tins (for a traditional touch, keep back a little of the dough, then roll it into small balls and put one on top of each brioche). Allow the dough to prove for 10–15 minutes, then bake for 12 minutes until brown.

5   To serve, gently heat the vanilla custard over a bain-marie, whisking continuously. Bring 6 tablespoons of the spiced plum sauce to simmering point in a saucepan. Unmould the hot brioches onto serving plates, then dust with icing sugar and spoon vanilla custard around one side of each brioche and spiced plum sauce around the other side.

BAKED BLOOD PLUM BRIOCHE WITH SPICED PLUM SAUCE AND VANILLA CUSTARD

GRILLED FIGS WITH LEMON VERBENA PANNA COTTA AND PISTACHIO NUTS

# GRILLED FIGS WITH LEMON VERBENA PANNA COTTA AND PISTACHIO NUTS

The late months of summer produce beautiful figs, heavily scented lemon verbena and fresh pistachio nuts, now grown in Victoria. The technique involved here is quite straight-forward – 'panna cotta' translates from the Italian as 'cooked cream', a cream that has been cooked with a chosen flavour and set with gelatine. The wonder of the dessert lies in the perfect symphony the flavours create. A fantastic late summer or early autumn dessert with minimal preparation.

18 perfect ripe figs
icing sugar
6 tablespoons lemon syrup (see Citrus Syrup page 8)
60 g fresh pistachio nuts, chopped

**PANNA COTTA**
750 ml thick (45 per cent) cream
250 ml milk
75 g fresh lemon verbena leaves
235 g castor sugar
3 gelatine leaves

1   To make the panna cotta, put the cream, milk, lemon verbena and 75 g of the castor sugar into a stainless steel saucepan and bring very slowly to simmering point, stirring occasionally, to allow the flavour of the verbena to infuse the cream mixture. This will take about 1 hour.

2   Soften the gelatine leaves in a little cold water, then wring out the excess water. Remove the cream mixture from the heat, then stir in the remaining 160 g castor sugar and the softened gelatine leaves until dissolved. Pass the cream mixture through a fine-meshed sieve or muslin into a clean bowl or jug and discard the lemon verbena. Pour the cream into 6 x 120 ml dariole moulds and refrigerate for at least 8 hours before serving.

3   To serve, preheat an overhead griller or salamander. Slice the figs in half lengthwise, then arrange them cut-side up on a baking tray and dust them liberally with icing sugar. Grill the figs until they become juicy and begin to colour.

4   Remove the panna cotta from the refrigerator. Dip each mould into hot water, one at a time, for 10 seconds, then invert onto a serving plate. The creams should slide out intact. Sit 6 grilled fig halves around each panna cotta, then spoon lemon syrup over the figs and pile the chopped pistachios on top of the figs and the creams. Serve immediately.

# LEMON CURD TARTS WITH LEMON CONFIT

1 quantity Lemon Curd (see
    page 15)
1 quantity Sweet Lemon Pastry
    (see page 23)

**LEMON CONFIT**
6 lemons
1 handful fresh lemon verbena
    leaves
1 litre Sugar Syrup (see page 8)
1 stick cinnamon
1 vanilla bean, split

The lemon is one of those ingredients that cries out to be included in a dessert menu, since acidity and sugar work in perfect harmony when balanced. Nothing beats a freshly baked lemon tart after lunch or a cone of lemon gelato after a fiery curry.

The culinary versatility of the lemon is renowned. In *Much Depends on Dinner* Margaret Visser writes: 'handy in size, available all year round, inexpensive, long lasting, and perfectly packaged in a tough skin which is as valuable as the juice it contains, a lemon is the ideal household implement, an honourable standard against which all patented inventions might be measured. A modern kitchen without a lemon in it is gravely ill-equipped.'

These tarts build on the flavour of the lemon, starting with the pastry, followed by the curd and then the confit. The lemon confit is a result of experimenting with the fruit after tasting one of the definitive dishes of Berowra Waters Inn, the lemon and citron dessert created by Gay Bilson and Janni Kyritsis. For an alternative taste and appearance, you could try making the tart shells with Chocolate Pastry (see page 24).

1   To make the lemon confit, slice the lemons finely into rounds, discarding the seeds and being careful not to rip the flesh. Put the sliced lemon into a bowl and pour over enough boiling water to cover, then allow to cool completely for 12 hours. Repeat this process twice – a total of 3 changes of water over 36 hours. By the end of the last soaking the lemon should be soft but have some resistance in the bite, and the flavour should still be tangy with a softened acidity.

2   Tie the lemon verbena in a muslin bag. Put the soaked lemon into a wide, heavy-based, stainless-steel pan with the lemon verbena, sugar syrup and cinnamon stick, then scrape in the seeds from the vanilla bean and add the bean itself. Cook over a low heat for 1 hour until the lemon is of a jelly-like consistency. Remove the cinnamon, vanilla bean and muslin bag. Allow the confit to cool and refrigerate until ready to use.

3   Make the lemon curd as instructed and allow it to cool.

4   Make the pastry and blind bake 6 small tart shells as instructed.

5   To serve, three-quarters fill each tart shell with lemon curd, then arrange some lemon confit carefully on top.

LEMON CURD TART WITH LEMON CONFIT

TOFFEE APPLE AND PINEAPPLE CHARLOTTE WITH STAR ANISE CUSTARD AND CANDIED PINEAPPLE WAFER

# TOFFEE APPLE AND PINEAPPLE CHARLOTTES WITH STAR ANISE CUSTARD AND CANDIED PINEAPPLE WAFERS

**T**his is a celebration of sugar and spice and all things nice – a heady mix of tropical sweetness! A charlotte is a French term given to a moulded dessert that usually comprises sponge and jelly layers, a rich custard filling and fruit. In this instance, I have taken artistic licence and used the charlotte mould and the principle of its assembly but for a different effect. Choose the smaller sweet pineapple referred to as a 'roughy' for this dessert.

1   Butter and sugar 6 x 200 ml charlotte moulds. Slice the toffee apple finely and line the moulds with it, working from the bottom up. Leave enough apple hanging over the edge of each mould so that it can be folded over the filling later on.

2   To make the charlotte filling, melt the ghee in a stainless steel frying pan. Add the diced pineapple and diced toffee apple and stir over moderate heat for a few minutes until slightly caramelised. Scrape the vanilla bean seeds into the pan, then add the bean itself and the star anise, calvados, honey and dark-brown sugar and stir to incorporate. Cook over a low heat for 15 minutes, stirring frequently. Remove the pan from the heat and discard the vanilla bean and star anise. Strain, reserving 200 ml cooking juices for the custard. Spoon the cooked fruit into the prepared moulds. Fold the apple slices over to cover the filling and wrap each mould in plastic film to secure. Refrigerate for 5 hours before serving.

3   To make the star anise custard, bring the cream and star anise to simmering point in a saucepan. Whisk the egg yolks and castor sugar in a bowl until pale and frothy. Slowly stir the reserved 200 ml juices from the cooked fruit into the egg mixture and then whisk in the hot cream. Stand the bowl over a bain-marie and cook, stirring, over a gentle heat until the mixture coats the back of a

spoon. Pass the custard through a fine-meshed sieve into a bowl, then press a piece of plastic film down onto the surface to prevent a skin forming and set aside until ready to use.

4   To make the candied pineapple wafers, melt the butter and liquid glucose in a bowl over a bain-marie. Combine the flour, castor sugar and candied pineapple in another bowl, then pour in the melted butter mixture and stir to incorporate. Allow to cool before proceeding.

5   Preheat the oven to 180°C and line a baking tray with baking paper. Roll the wafer mixture into small balls, using a teaspoonful for each one, then cook 2 at a time for 5 minutes or until caramel-coloured. Remove the tray from the oven and allow the wafers to cool for 15–20 seconds, then cut each one while warm and pliable into rounds using a 9 cm pastry cutter. Discard the excess. Let the wafers cool and firm on the tray, then transfer to an airtight container until ready to use.

6   To serve, reheat the custard gently in a bowl over a bain-marie, whisking continuously. Steam the charlottes gently for 5 minutes, then carefully turn them out of their moulds onto serving plates. Ladle some hot custard around the base of each charlotte, then sit a biscuit on top and serve immediately.

1 quantity Toffee Apple (see page 13)

**CHARLOTTE FILLING**
100 g ghee
1 ripe roughy pineapple, cored and finely diced
⅓ quantity Toffee Apple (see page 13), diced
1 vanilla bean, split
2 star anise
25 ml calvados
35 g honey
30 g dark-brown sugar

**STAR ANISE CUSTARD**
375 ml pouring (35 per cent) cream
1 star anise, broken
6 large egg yolks
100 g castor sugar

**CANDIED PINEAPPLE WAFERS**
50 g unsalted butter
45 g liquid glucose
45 g plain flour
90 g castor sugar
2 teaspoons finely diced candied pineapple

# BLOOD-ORANGE CREAM AND MERINGUE TARTS WITH STRAWBERRIES

1 quantity Sweet Orange Pastry
   (see page 22)
icing sugar
12 perfect large strawberries,
   sliced
6 tablespoons blood-orange
   syrup (see Citrus Syrup
   page 8)

**BLOOD-ORANGE CREAM**
250 ml thick (45 per cent) cream
zest of 1 blood orange
6 egg yolks
50 g castor sugar
125 ml strained fresh blood-
   orange juice
1 gelatine leaf

**MERINGUES**
75 g egg whites
75 g castor sugar
½ teaspoon cream of tartar

**B**lood oranges have a very short season as they drop their fruit in one go, usually around the end of August, so have to be dealt with quickly. Sweeter and less acidic than the more usual oranges, they are not to be missed, so freeze the juice and think of a million ways of using it.

The idea for this dessert comes from the well-known lemon meringue pie, while its presentation was inspired by a lemon tart I saw in New York at City Bakery, a wonderful pâtisserie and bread shop near Union Square.

**1**   Prepare the pastry and blind bake 6 small tart shells as instructed.

**2**   To make the blood-orange cream, bring the cream to simmering point in a saucepan with the blood-orange zest. Whisk the egg yolks and castor sugar in a bowl until pale and creamy, then add the blood-orange juice and whisk in the hot cream. Stand the bowl over a bain-marie and cook, whisking continuously, until thick.

**3**   Soften the gelatine leaf in a little cold water, then squeeze out the excess water and stir the gelatine into the custard until dissolved. Pass the custard through a fine-meshed sieve into a bowl and cool over ice in the refrigerator. Press a piece of plastic film down onto the custard to prevent a skin forming and refrigerate until ready to use.

**4**   To make the meringues, whisk the egg whites until stiff, then slowly add the castor sugar, still beating. Fold in the cream of tartar. Set out 6 egg rings on a baking tray lined with baking paper, then line the inside of each ring with a strip of baking paper as well. Spoon the meringue mixture into a piping bag fitted with a plain nozzle and pipe it into the rings, finishing each one with a little peak. Freeze for up to 2 hours until ready to serve.

**5**   Preheat the oven to 180°C. To serve, dust the meringues with icing sugar and bake for 6 minutes until they begin to colour. While the meringues are cooking, fill each freshly baked tart shell with the blood-orange cream, then arrange the sliced strawberries on the cream with their pointed ends jutting out over the edge of the pastry and put the tarts on serving plates. Remove the meringues from the oven and take off the metal collars and paper wraps, then dust with a little extra icing sugar, if desired. Carefully slide a meringue on top of the strawberries, then spoon blood-orange syrup around the tarts and serve.

BLOOD-ORANGE CREAM AND MERINGUE TART WITH STRAWBERRIES

BRANDIED CHERRY JELLY WITH COCONUT BAVAROIS AND CHOCOLATE WAFER

# BRANDIED CHERRY JELLIES WITH COCONUT BAVAROIS AND CHOCOLATE WAFERS

One of my favourite obsessions is to dream up adult versions of the popular sweet treats and memories of childhood. My work takes those basic flavours, gives them a highly refined and sophisticated application and introduces grown-up textures and flavours to seduce our palates. This is my interpretation of the Cherry Ripe chocolate bar.

1   Make the chocolate fudge cake as instructed. Wrap it in plastic film and store it at room temperature until ready to use.

2   To make the coconut bavarois, infuse the shredded coconut in the milk over a low heat until simmering point is reached. The lower the heat, the less the milk will reduce and the more flavour will be extracted from the coconut – infusing for an hour is ideal.

3   Whisk the egg yolks and castor sugar in a bowl until light and frothy. Pour the hot milk and coconut slowly into the egg mixture, whisking continuously to prevent curdling. Stand the bowl over a bain-marie and cook over a medium heat, whisking continuously, until the mixture coats the back of a spoon.

4   Soften the gelatine leaf in a little cold water, then wring out the excess water and stir the gelatine into the custard until dissolved. Remove the bowl from the heat and pass the custard through a fine-meshed sieve into another bowl, pressing on the coconut to extract as much milk as possible, then discard the coconut. Stand the bowl over ice and continue to whisk to cool the custard.

5   When the custard is cool, whisk in the whipped cream. Half-fill 6 × 120 ml dariole moulds, leaving room for the jelly and cake layers. Refrigerate the moulds until the bavarois has set (it will take about 1 hour) before adding the remaining layers.

6   While the bavarois is setting, make the cherry jelly. Bring the preserving liquid to simmering point in a stainless steel saucepan. Soften the gelatine leaves in a little cold water, then wring out the excess water and stir the gelatine into the hot liquid until dissolved. Pass the hot cherry jelly through a fine-meshed sieve into a clean bowl and allow to cool but not set.

7   When the bavarois has set and the jelly mixture has cooled, remove the moulds from the refrigerator and stand them on a tray. Sit 5 brandied cherries on each bavarois layer and pour in the cool jelly to cover them until 1 cm from the top. Refrigerate the moulds until the jelly has set – this will take about 45 minutes.

8   To complete the desserts, cut 6 × 1 cm thick rounds of the chocolate fudge cake using a pastry cutter the same diameter as the moulds. It may be necessary to trim the cake

1 Chocolate Fudge Cake (see page 28)
30 Brandied Cherries (see page 12), drained
1 quantity Cherry Syrup (see page 8)

### COCONUT BAVAROIS
40 g shredded coconut
175 ml milk
3 large egg yolks
110 g castor sugar
1 gelatine leaf
200 ml thick (45 per cent) cream, whipped

### CHERRY JELLY
185 ml Brandied Cherries liquid (see page 12)
1½ gelatine leaves

### CHOCOLATE WAFERS
55 g unsalted butter
45 g liquid glucose
50 g dark couverture chocolate
45 g plain flour
40 g Dutch cocoa powder
90 g castor sugar

►

rounds so they are even. Sit the cake on top of the jelly layer in each mould, then press down gently and cover with plastic film. Refrigerate for at least 3 hours before serving.

**9** To make the chocolate wafers, mix the butter, liquid glucose and chocolate in a bowl over a bain-marie until softened. In another bowl, combine the flour, cocoa powder and castor sugar. Stir the chocolate mixture into the dry ingredients until well combined. Wrap the mixture in plastic film and refrigerate until it becomes firm, about 2 hours.

**10** Preheat the oven to 180°C. Cook 2 teaspoonfuls of the wafer mixture on a baking tray lined with baking paper for 5 minutes. Remove the tray from the oven, then cover the hot and bubbling wafers with another sheet of baking paper and press with a flat-bottomed glass to expel any excess butter. This gives the wafers a smooth appearance and fine texture. (Don't be tempted to cook any more than 2 wafers at a time as the mixture spreads on the tray as it cooks, and you have to work deftly once the wafers are cooked as they begin to set almost immediately.) Continue the process until you have cooked enough wafers. Reserve the remaining mixture for later use (it will keep, refrigerated, for a month).

**11** To serve, suspend each mould briefly in hot water and carefully turn out onto a serving plate. Spoon some cherry syrup around and lean a chocolate wafer against each 'cherry ripe', then serve immediately.

# TUILE CONES WITH CARAMELISED APPLE, GINGER CUSTARD AND TOKAY CARAMEL

**T**his dessert was the fabulous finale at the banquet dinner for the 1996 Symposium of Australian Gastronomy in the Sydney Opera House. My close colleague Lew Kathreptis and I were given the enormous and thrilling task of putting the grand dinner together. Our instruction was that we were to focus on the theme of the conference: Food and Power. We wanted more than a mere meal; we envisaged a show of power, one that reflected our place in time. We enlisted the help of dear friend and art director Mary Paul to complement each course with a performance that illustrated an aspect of power. The entire evening was one of spectacle, especially the dessert and its accompanying performance, and will live on in the memories of those who attended. The seduction of the apple started with Adam and Eve, so blame them!

Performances aside, the flavours and textures of this dessert are fabulous in their own right. Note that the ginger custard and the tuile biscuits can be made in advance, leaving little to do on the day except create your own spectacle!

1 quantity Toffee Apple (see page 13)
75 ml liqueur tokay
1 quantity Tuile Biscuit mixture (see page 18)

### THICK GINGER CUSTARD CREAM
350 ml thick (45 per cent) cream
1 tablespoon minced fresh ginger
6 large egg yolks
60 g castor sugar
½ gelatine leaf

**1** Make the toffee apple as instructed. Remove the apple from the baking dish while still warm and store on a sheet of baking paper until ready to use. Reserve the caramel in the baking tray.

**2** Add the liqueur tokay to the warm caramel in the baking tray and cook over direct heat for a minute until amalgamated. Pour the tokay caramel through a fine-meshed sieve into a jug and leave at room temperature until ready to serve.

**3** To make the thick ginger custard cream, infuse the cream and ginger by bringing them gently to simmering point in a saucepan. Whisk the egg yolks and castor sugar in a bowl until light and frothy, then slowly pour in the hot cream, whisking continuously. Stand the bowl over a bain-marie and cook, stirring, until the custard becomes thick.

**4** Soften the gelatine leaf in a little cold water, then wring out the excess water and stir the gelatine into the thick custard until dissolved. Remove the bowl from the heat and pour the custard through a fine-meshed sieve into another bowl, pushing with a wooden spoon. This will remove the unwanted ginger flesh and any tiny lumps that may have formed during cooking. Cool the custard over ice, stirring regularly to prevent a skin forming. When cool, spoon into a plastic container and seal until ready to use. (This custard can be prepared a day or two ahead.)

**5** Make and chill the tuile biscuit mixture as instructed. Preheat the oven to 160°C and

▶

line the outside of 6 x 12 cm high and 4 cm wide metal pastry horn moulds with baking paper. Fold the excess paper into the hollow centre to secure the lining.

**6**  Bake the chilled tuile sheet for 4 minutes, then remove it from the oven. It should be just set but not cooked or coloured. Using a semi-circular template the same depth as the metal moulds, cut 6 shapes using a sharp knife, then remove the unwanted mixture and return the tray to the oven for 3 minutes. The biscuit shapes should now be cooked and pale golden brown. Remove the tray from the oven and work quickly to wrap each biscuit around the moulds. Lie the cones on their

seams to set for 1–2 minutes, then stand them upright. Allow the cones to cool, then store them on their moulds in an airtight container until ready to use.

**7**  Carefully remove the cones from the lined moulds just before they are needed. To assemble the dessert, arrange 4 slices of the toffee apple in the centre of each plate. Upturn each tuile cone and half-fill it with thick ginger custard cream, then add a piece of apple and fill the remaining space with more custard. Stand the cones on the apple slices and add a couple more slices to the top of each one. Drizzle the tokay caramel over the apple at the base and serve immediately.

TUILE CONE WITH CARAMELISED APPLE, GINGER CUSTARD AND TOKAY CARAMEL

BAKED QUINCE AND CINNAMON BRIOCHE WITH CRÈME FRAÎCHE

# BAKED QUINCE AND CINNAMON BRIOCHE WITH CRÈME FRAÎCHE

**A**s quinces cook with sugar or honey they change colour, the sugar transforming the pale, woody flesh into something rich, red and tender. Another version of this dessert is to work some of the cooked quince into the brioche dough as it is being rolled ready for baking to give added textural dimension. Prepared this way, the brioche can also be served simply as a tea cake.

1   Preheat the oven to 120°C. To bake the quinces, peel the fruit and cut it in half lengthwise, leaving the cores intact. In a wide, heavy-based pan, bring the quince syrup, sugar syrup, cinnamon sticks, vanilla bean and mace to boiling point on the stove. Add the quince halves and ensure they are covered by the liquid. Press a piece of baking paper down onto the fruit to keep it submerged, then cover with a lid or a double sheet of foil and bake in the oven for 6–8 hours until the quinces are soft to the touch and red in colour.

2   Remove the cooked fruit from the liquid and set aside, then reduce the liquid over a high heat on the stove until it reaches a syrupy consistency. Remove the cores from the quince.

3   To serve, preheat an overhead griller. Butter the brioche slices and sprinkle with cinnamon and castor sugar and lightly toast under the griller. Arrange 2 baked quince halves and a slice of brioche on each serving plate, then spoon some of the reduced cooking liquid over the quince and serve with the crème fraîche.

10 g unsalted butter
6 slices Cinnamon Brioche (see page 27)
½ teaspoon ground cinnamon
1 teaspoon castor sugar
6 tablespoons crème fraîche

**BAKED QUINCES**

6 quinces
200 ml Quince Syrup (see page 9)
1 litre Sugar Syrup (see page 8)
2 sticks cinnamon
1 vanilla bean, split
½ teaspoon whole mace

# CARAMELISED COCONUT CREAMS WITH MANGO, LIME SYRUP AND COCONUT TUILES

3 ripe mangoes
6 tablespoons lime syrup (see Citrus Syrup page 8)
3 tablespoons freshly shredded coconut

**COCONUT CREAMS**
300 g castor sugar
50 ml water
200 ml coconut milk
30 g freshly grated coconut, lightly toasted
75 g coconut sugar, shaved
350 ml thick (45 per cent) cream
2 eggs
6 egg yolks

**COCONUT TUILES**
6 tablespoons Tuile Biscuit mixture (see page 18)
3 teaspoons shredded coconut

This is a variation of a caramelised cream, this time using the tropical flavours of the highly perfumed mango and the rich creaminess of the coconut, a natural partnership.

Coconut sugar is similar to palm sugar as it comes in block form and is caramel in colour but it has an intense coconut flavour. It is available from Asian food stores.

1   To make the coconut creams, make a caramel by boiling the castor sugar and water over a high heat without stirring. Pour the hot caramel into 6 x 150 ml dariole moulds, working quickly as the caramel will continue to cook and will darken. Tilt the moulds to ensure each is evenly lined with caramel, then discard any excess and allow to cool.

2   Preheat the oven to 150°C. Bring the coconut milk, toasted coconut, coconut sugar and cream to simmering point in a saucepan over a low heat. Whisk the eggs and egg yolks in a bowl until pale and frothy, then slowly whisk in the hot cream mixture. Pass the mixture through a fine-meshed sieve into a jug, then fill the prepared moulds. Stand the creams in a water bath and cook for 45 minutes or until set. Remove the creams from the water bath and allow to cool, then refrigerate for at least 5 hours before serving.

3   To make the coconut tuiles, butter and flour a baking tray. Spread the tuile biscuit mixture onto the tray in a thin, even layer, then sprinkle with the shredded coconut and refrigerate for 1 hour to set.

4   Preheat the oven to 160°C. Bake the chilled tuile sheet for 5 minutes or until pale golden. Remove the tray from the oven and quickly cut out triangles using a large, sharp knife, then transfer the tuiles to a wire rack to set. Store in an airtight container between sheets of baking paper until ready to use.

5   To serve, slice the cheeks of the mangoes from the seeds, then peel these and slice a bit off the curved surface and sit a mango cheek on each serving plate. Suspend each coconut cream in hot water for 30 seconds, then carefully turn out onto the mango, letting the caramel pour over the cream. Spoon lime syrup around the mango and sprinkle shredded coconut on top of the creams, then add a coconut tuile to each plate and serve.

CARAMELISED COCONUT CREAM WITH MANGO, LIME SYRUP AND COCONUT TUILE

BLACK FIGS WITH HONEY MOUSSE AND HAZELNUT SPONGE

# BLACK FIGS WITH HONEY MOUSSE AND HAZELNUT SPONGE

Perfectly ripe black genoan figs, the figs with the luscious purple centres, are partnered perfectly here by the sweetness of honey and a nutty meringue-like sponge in a voluptuous dessert that is as sensual to look at as it is to eat.

Figs are part of our mythology and evoke many images. In *The Cook's Companion* Stephanie Alexander writes that 'a fully ripe fig eaten warm from the tree is an emotional experience'. Take that experience one step further and cook this dessert – you may need to describe it with the evocative language of D.H. Lawrence!

6 large perfect ripe black figs, thinly sliced

**HAZELNUT SPONGE**
3 large eggs, separated
125 g castor sugar
125 g ground hazelnuts

**FIG JELLY**
12 ripe black figs
200 ml Sugar Syrup (see page 8)
75 ml cassis
2 gelatine leaves

**HONEY MOUSSE**
4 egg yolks
100 g castor sugar
320 ml milk
60 g honey
2½ gelatine leaves
250 ml thick (45 per cent) cream

1   To make the hazelnut sponge, preheat the oven to 180°C and grease and line a 24 cm x 20 cm cake tin. Beat the egg yolks with half the castor sugar in a bowl until light and frothy, then stir in the ground hazelnuts. In another bowl, whisk the egg whites until stiff and slowly beat in the remaining castor sugar. Fold the two mixtures together gently, then spoon into the prepared tin and smooth the top before baking for 30 minutes. Remove the tin from the oven and turn the cake out onto a wire rack to cool.

2   To make the fig jelly, chop the figs and stew them in the sugar syrup and cassis over a low heat for 30 minutes until the mixture resembles a lumpy sauce. In the meantime, soak the gelatine leaves in cold water until softened, then wring out the excess water. Strain the hot fig juice through a fine-meshed sieve, then discard the solids. Measure out 250 ml juice (reserve the rest for serving as a sauce) and stir in the gelatine until dissolved. Strain the hot jelly into a jug, then pour it into 6 x 200 ml dariole moulds and allow to set (the jelly will be about 5 mm deep). Once the jelly has just set, carefully lie a slice of fig on each jelly layer, then line the sides of each mould with 3 more slices of fig. Refrigerate the moulds until you are ready to fill them.

3   To make the honey mousse, whisk the egg yolks and castor sugar in a bowl. Bring the milk and honey to simmering point in a saucepan, then whisk this slowly into the egg mixture. Stand the bowl over a bain-marie and stir over gentle heat until the mixture coats the back of a spoon. Soften the gelatine in a little cold water, then wring out the excess water and stir the gelatine into the custard until dissolved. Pass the custard through a fine-meshed sieve into a bowl and cool over ice, whisking constantly to keep it aerated as it cools. Whip the cream until stiff peaks form and fold it into the cooled custard. Spoon the mousse into the prepared moulds until 1 cm from the rim, then refrigerate until set, about 4 hours.

4   Using a pastry cutter, cut out 6 x 1 cm thick rounds of hazelnut sponge the same diameter as the moulds, then position the cake on the mousse so that it is level with the top of the moulds. Cover with plastic film to secure and refrigerate for at least 3 hours before serving.

5   To serve, suspend each mould in hot water for 30 seconds, then turn out onto a serving plate and spoon some of the reserved fig syrup around the base.

# PARAMOUNT PEACH MELBA

500 g perfect raspberries

150 ml Raspberry Sauce (see
    page 10)

½ quantity Thick Vanilla Cream
    (see page 16)

**SAUTERNES-POACHED
PEACHES**

250 ml sauternes

100 ml riesling

250 ml Sugar Syrup (see page 8)

25 ml vanilla essence

100 ml strained fresh orange
    juice

zest of 1 orange

zest of 1 lemon

6 large yellow slipstone peaches

This dessert takes its cue from the dish invented by Auguste Escoffier at the turn of the twentieth century in honour of the Australian opera singer Dame Nellie Melba. I use the same flavours but give it a different interpretation on the plate. A perfectly poached peach, with a secret heart of fresh raspberries, sits regally on a bed of vanilla cream surrounded by raspberry sauce. This dessert is a fast one to put together as long as each component has been prepared beforehand.

1   To make the sauternes-poached peaches, bring all the ingredients except the peaches to a boil, then reduce to a simmer and add the fruit. Gently poach the peaches until soft and the skins are just starting to split. Remove the peaches from the syrup and allow to cool. Reserve the syrup for another time (it keeps well refrigerated and the peach flavour intensifies with repeated use).

2   To assemble, peel the peaches, then split each one in half and remove the stone carefully. Stuff each peach with raspberries, then push the halves together.

3   Spread 25 ml raspberry sauce evenly over the centre of each serving plate, then spoon the vanilla cream into the middle of this.

4   Glaze each peach with the cooking syrup and then sit it in the centre of the vanilla cream. Repeat with the remaining peaches and dot a few raspberries around the base of each one, if you like. Serve immediately.

PARAMOUNT PEACH MELBA

GLAZED QUINCE TART WITH VANILLA CREAM AND QUINCE SYRUP

# GLAZED QUINCE TARTS WITH
# VANILLA CREAM AND QUINCE SYRUP

The cuisines of the Mediterranean and Middle East use quinces in many ways but it is their cooking with sugar or honey I am most attracted by and practised at. Cooking and care turn these highly perfumed specimens into taste treats. And it is with a passionate heart and an understanding of the nature of the quince that a cook must then tackle the task of making them into a delectable dessert.

1 quantity Sweet Pastry (see page 22)
6 Poached Quince halves (see page 11)
6 tablespoons Thick Vanilla Cream (see page 16)
6 teaspoons demerara sugar
6 tablespoons Quince Syrup (see page 9)

1  Prepare the pastry and blind bake 6 small tart shells as instructed.

2  Preheat the oven to 150°C. To assemble the tarts, slice the quince halves and arrange the fruit across the bottom of each tart shell, then warm in the oven for 5 minutes. Spoon the vanilla cream over the warm quince until the tart shells are full, then sprinkle with demerara sugar and caramelise with a blow torch (don't be tempted to use a griller instead – it will not be hot enough and the cream will split).

3  Carefully remove the tarts from their tins and put them on serving plates. Spoon 1 tablespoon quince syrup around each tart and serve immediately.

# ALMOND MACAROON NECTARINES WITH SAUTERNES CUSTARD

6 large ripe nectarines
50 g castor sugar

**SAUTERNES CUSTARD**
250 ml pouring (35 per cent)
    cream
125 ml sauternes
4 large egg yolks
75 g castor sugar

**ALMOND MACAROON
STUFFING**
100 g almond Macaroons (see
    page 141)
50 g fresh Kakadu bread dates,
    stoned and finely chopped
20 g minced candied citron
½ teaspoon minced candied
    ginger
25 g unsalted butter, softened
freshly grated nutmeg

Macaroons, little sweet biscuits originally from Italy but popularised and made famous in north-eastern France, have a wonderful chewy texture that works perfectly with cooked nectarines. The macaroon stuffing used in this dessert, made to resemble the stones that have been removed from the fruit, offers a contrast in texture to the smooth, firm and juicy nectarine flesh. The recipe works just as well with other stone fruits, such as peaches or apricots.

1   To make the sauternes custard, heat the cream and sauternes in separate stainless steel saucepans until simmering, making sure neither boils. Whisk the egg yolks and castor sugar in a bowl until light and frothy. Pour the warm cream into the egg mixture in a slow, thin stream, whisking gently. Repeat the process with the warm sauternes. Stand the bowl over a bain-marie and cook, whisking, until the mixture coats the back of a spoon. Pass the custard through a fine-meshed sieve into a clean bowl. Press a piece of plastic film down onto the surface of the custard to stop a skin forming and set aside.

2   To make the almond macaroon stuffing, crumble the macaroon biscuits in a food processor. Add the remaining ingredients and mix thoroughly by hand. Keep refrigerated until ready to use.

3   Prepare the nectarines just before serving to avoid discoloration. Preheat an overhead griller. Cut each nectarine in half and remove the stones carefully without ripping the flesh. Stand the halves on a baking tray, cut-side up.

4   Roll the stuffing into balls the size of the nectarine stones and place one in each cavity. Sprinkle the nectarines with the castor sugar and grill until the sugar has caramelised and the nectarines are glazed.

5   To serve, put 2 nectarine halves into each shallow serving bowl and pour the warm sauternes custard around the fruit. (Gently reheat the custard over a bain-marie if necessary, whisking continuously.) Serve immediately.

ALMOND MACAROON NECTARINES WITH SAUTERNES CUSTARD

CARAMELISED MAPLE CREAM WITH TOFFEE APPLE AND CARAMEL WAFER

# CARAMELISED MAPLE CREAMS WITH TOFFEE APPLE AND CARAMEL WAFERS

After a recent visit to Canada, I had to transport one taste sensation back with me. Yes, I lugged back a large quantity of pure AA-grade maple syrup I had purchased at the wonderful Granville Island food market in Vancouver! I then reworked the caramelised cream recipe to incorporate this luscious syrup.

1   To make the maple creams, preheat the oven to 150°C. Make a caramel by boiling the castor sugar and water over a high heat without stirring. Pour the hot caramel into 6 x 150 ml dariole moulds, working quickly as the caramel will continue to cook and will darken. Tilt the moulds to ensure each is evenly lined with caramel, then discard any excess and allow the caramel to cool.

2   Bring the cream, milk and maple syrup to simmering point in a saucepan over a medium heat. Whisk the eggs and egg yolks in a bowl, then slowly pour in the hot cream, whisking continuously. Pour the cream through a fine-meshed sieve into a jug, then fill the prepared moulds. Remove any surface bubbles using a teaspoon. Bake the creams in a water bath for 45 minutes or until just set. Remove the water bath from the oven and allow the creams to cool in it. Remove the creams from the water, then refrigerate them on a tray, covered with plastic film, for 5 hours before serving.

3   To make the caramel wafers, butter and flour a baking tray and spread the tuile biscuit mixture in 6 x 8 cm even rounds (it may be necessary to make a template). Refrigerate for 1 hour before baking.

4   Preheat the oven to 160°C. Bake the chilled wafers for 5–6 minutes until caramel-coloured. Remove the tray from the oven and slide the wafers carefully onto a wire rack. Make a pale caramel by boiling the castor sugar and water over a high heat without stirring. Using a spoon, drizzle the warm caramel back and forth over the wafers, making a series of lines across their surface. Allow to cool and set completely. Store the wafers between layers of baking paper in an airtight container until ready to use.

5   Make the toffee apple as instructed and set aside.

6   To serve, suspend each maple cream in hot water for 30 seconds and then carefully turn out onto a serving plate, letting the caramel pour over the cream. Arrange 4 toffee apple slices around the base of each cream and spoon some maple syrup over them. Sit the caramel wafers across the maple creams and serve immediately.

½ quantity Toffee Apple (see page 13)
6 teaspoons pure maple syrup

**MAPLE CREAMS**
300 g castor sugar
100 ml water
500 ml thick (45 per cent) cream
100 ml milk
125 ml pure maple syrup
2 eggs
6 egg yolks

**CARAMEL WAFERS**
6 tablespoons Tuile Biscuit mixture (see page 18)
200 g castor sugar
50 ml water

# STEAMED BLACKBERRY SPONGE PUDDINGS WITH VANILLA CUSTARD AND BLACKBERRY SAUCE

½ quantity Vanilla Custard (see page 17)

**BLACKBERRY SAUCE**
500 g blackberries
75 ml Sugar Syrup (see page 8)
1 teaspoon strained fresh lemon
juice

**SPONGE PUDDINGS**
250 g blackberries
3 large eggs, separated
100 g castor sugar
½ vanilla bean
20 g butter, melted
150 ml buttermilk
190 g self-raising flour, sifted
½ teaspoon baking powder

**A** hot pudding on a menu is always a winner and the combination of a hot, light sponge saturated with the sweet tartness of blackberries puts this one in the serious comfort zone. It's what I call a good old-fashioned dessert.

1   Make the vanilla custard as instructed, then press plastic film down onto the surface to prevent a skin forming and set aside.

2   To make the blackberry sauce, purée 250 g of the blackberries with the sugar syrup and lemon juice in a food processor until smooth. Pass the sauce through a fine-meshed sieve and discard the solids. Keep refrigerated until ready to use.

3   To make the sponge puddings, preheat the oven to 180°C. Butter and sugar 6 × 200 ml pudding moulds, then divide the blackberries between the moulds. Beat the egg whites until stiff peaks form. In another bowl, whisk the egg yolks and castor sugar until light and frothy. Scrape the seeds from the vanilla bean into the egg yolk mixture, then stir in the melted butter and the buttermilk. Gently mix in the flour and baking powder to form a batter, then gently fold in the egg whites. Spoon the batter into the prepared moulds until almost full. Stand the moulds in a water bath and cover the whole water bath with foil. Cook the puddings for 30 minutes, rotating the moulds at 15 minutes to ensure even cooking, then remove them from the water bath. Allow the puddings to sit for 4–5 minutes before turning them out.

4   To serve, warm the remaining 250 g blackberries in the sauce and reheat the custard over a bain-marie, stirring gently. Turn the puddings out of their moulds onto serving plates, using a paring knife to loosen the edges. Sit some blackberries from the sauce on top of each pudding, then ladle hot vanilla custard around the puddings and add a splash of the blackberry sauce. Serve immediately.

STEAMED BLACKBERRY SPONGE PUDDING WITH VANILLA CUSTARD AND BLACKBERRY SAUCE

# ICE-CREAMS AND SORBETS

The making of good ice-cream and sorbet is quite straightforward. It is the ability to transform ingredients into conceptual artworks based on principles of design and construction that takes the cook into another realm and level of preparation – a new world of cooking and science. Ice-cream and sorbet construction is a direct response to and understanding of alchemy.

Like the famous French chef Antonin Carême, who perfected the art of ice-cream moulding and sculpture in the early nineteenth century, I also believe in luxurious excess and grandiose gestures with food. Doing so gives a formality, a sense of occasion to food, and allows the cook's personality to shine through. It encourages folly, where artistry and a sense of architecture are revealed without compromising flavour.

Credit for the art and alchemy of ice-cream construction in modern Australian cooking as practised by me and many other restaurant chefs lies with fellow chef Phillip Searle, my previous employer and mentor. In the early 1980s he created a spectacular chequerboard of star anise ice-cream, pineapple sorbet and liquorice ice-cream that has become a benchmark of perfection in taste, construction and design. Nothing I have eaten in the best restaurants of the world comes close to its ethereal and divine presence. It is from this starting point that I draw my inspiration and desire to achieve the best work of which I am capable.

# ICED PYRAMIDS OF MANGO SORBET AND TOASTED COCONUT ICE-CREAM WITH COCONUT WAFERS

1½ quantities Mango Sorbet (see page 114)
1 quantity Coconut Wafer mixture (see page 135)

**TOASTED COCONUT ICE-CREAM**
750 ml pouring (35 per cent) cream
500 ml milk
75 g coconut flakes, toasted
200 g coconut sugar, shaved
12 large egg yolks

Marco Pierre White, the famed London chef, is the first person in modern professional cooking I am aware of to have constructed ice-cream in the shape of a pyramid. His signature dessert is based on a nougat ice-cream concealed beneath perfectly formed almond praline biscuits and served with passionfruit. It tastes as dreamy as it looks.

The stainless steel moulds I use are French, but the effect can be duplicated easily by using cardboard moulds lined with baking paper.

Coconut sugar is similar to palm sugar as it comes in block form and is caramel in colour but it has an intense coconut flavour. It is available from Asian food stores.

1   Position 6 x 9 cm x 8 cm metal pyramid moulds upside down in a frame to keep them even and steady (I sit them in a tin or sometimes cut holes in a small foam or cardboard box to hold them).

2   Make the mango sorbet as instructed. Half-fill the moulds with the mango sorbet and freeze for 2 hours until firm.

3   To make the toasted coconut ice-cream, infuse the cream, milk, coconut flakes and coconut sugar in a saucepan over a very low heat until simmering point is reached. Whisk the egg yolks in a bowl until pale and frothy, then whisk in the hot cream mixture. Stand the bowl over a bain-marie and cook, stirring, until the mixture coats the back of a spoon. Pass the custard through a fine-meshed sieve into a bowl and discard the solids. Allow to cool, then churn in an ice-cream machine according to the manufacturer's instructions.

4   Fill the moulds with the toasted coconut ice-cream, using a spatula to smooth the surface. Freeze for 5 hours or overnight.

5   Make the coconut wafer mixture as instructed, then preheat the oven to 180°C and line a baking tray with baking paper. Press 2 tablespoons of the mixture onto the centre of the tray. Cover the mixture with another piece of baking paper and flatten with a rolling pin. Remove the top sheet of paper and bake the biscuit for 6 minutes or until golden. Remove the tray from the oven and allow the biscuit to cool for 1 minute, then cut out triangular biscuits to fit over the surfaces of the ice-cream pyramids (see the photograph opposite). Use a large, sharp knife and cut with precision and firmness. Work quickly before the biscuit cools and sets, when it becomes impossible to cut without breaking. Repeat the process until you have 12 biscuits. Store the biscuits in an airtight container between layers of paper until ready to use.

6   To serve, if you have used metal moulds, run them under hot water for a few seconds, then carefully slide each ice-cream out onto a cold plate and smooth the surfaces with a wet knife. (Cardboard moulds can just be cut away from the ice-cream and the baking paper removed.) Sit 2 coconut wafers on opposite surfaces so that the points cross each other at the top of the pyramid. Sometimes I serve this ice-cream with a little puddle of lime syrup (see Citrus Syrup on page 8).

ICED PYRAMID OF MANGO SORBET AND TOASTED COCONUT ICE-CREAM WITH COCONUT WAFERS

TROPICAL TUTTI-FRUTTI ICE-CREAM SLICE

# TROPICAL TUTTI-FRUTTI

# ICE-CREAM SLICE

This ice-cream, a careful selection of summer flavours, is ideal after spicy or rich food. Note that I also run a squiggle of papaya sorbet through the pineapple layer when preparing this for the restaurant – see the photograph opposite.

1 quantity Pineapple Sorbet (see page 114)

½ quantity Passionfruit Ice-cream (see page 114)

**RED PAPAYA SORBET**

100 g castor sugar

50 ml strained fresh lime juice

500 ml strained fresh red papaya purée

100 ml liquid glucose

**STRAWBERRY GUAVA ICE-CREAM**

270 g castor sugar

350 ml strained fresh strawberry guava purée

75 g liquid glucose

500 ml milk

6 large egg yolks

500 ml pouring (35 per cent) cream

1   Make the pineapple sorbet as instructed, then fill a hinged 32 cm × 4 cm cylindrical mould and press it shut. Freeze for at least 5 hours until very firm.

2   Remove the mould from the freezer and run it under hot water for a few seconds, then turn the pineapple sorbet log out onto a foil-lined board. Freeze for 30 minutes.

3   To make the red papaya sorbet, whisk the castor sugar and lime juice into the papaya purée until the sugar has dissolved. Melt the liquid glucose in a bowl over a bain-marie, then stir it thoroughly into the purée. Churn in an ice-cream machine according to the manufacturer's instructions.

4   Using a small palette knife, 'paint' a very thin layer of papaya sorbet over the pineapple sorbet log. Freeze for 2 hours until firm.

5   To make the strawberry guava ice-cream, whisk 70 g of the castor sugar into the guava purée until dissolved. Melt the liquid glucose in a bowl over a bain-marie, then stir it thoroughly into the purée. Bring the milk to simmering point in a saucepan. Whisk the egg yolks and remaining 200 g castor sugar in a bowl until pale and creamy, then slowly whisk in the hot milk. Stand the bowl over a bain-marie and cook, stirring, until the mixture coats the back of a spoon, then allow to cool. Pass the custard through a fine-meshed sieve into a bowl, then stir in the cream and sweetened purée. Churn in an ice-cream machine according to the manufacturer's instructions.

6   Line a 32 cm × 8 cm × 8 cm rectangular mould with baking paper, making sure the paper extends beyond the tin (this will help you remove the ice-cream from the mould later on). Half-fill the lined mould with strawberry guava ice-cream. While the ice-cream is still soft and pliable, sit the sorbet log on the ice-cream layer – the log should sink in a little and the ice-cream should come halfway up its sides. Tap the mould firmly to ensure there are no air bubbles. Freeze for 3 hours.

7   Make the passionfruit ice-cream as instructed. Fill the mould with the passionfruit ice-cream, then tap the mould to remove any air bubbles and freeze for at least 10 hours.

8   To complete the ice-cream assembly, churn the remaining papaya sorbet again and paint a 5 mm layer over the exposed surface of the passionfruit ice-cream. Return the mould to the freezer for 2 hours.

9   Run the mould under hot water for a few seconds, then turn the ice-cream log out onto a foil-lined board, using the paper lining to slide the ice-cream from its mould. Remove the paper from the ice-cream. Return the log to the freezer on the board for 30 minutes.

10   Churn the remaining papaya sorbet again, then paint a 5 mm layer over the remaining 3 ice-cream surfaces. Freeze for another 2 hours.

11   To serve, cut the ice-cream into 2 cm thick slices using a hot, wet, sharp knife and lie each slice on a cold plate.

# PARAMOUNT SPLICE

**PINEAPPLE SORBET**

75 g castor sugar

500 ml strained fresh pineapple
   juice

100 g liquid glucose

**MANGO SORBET**

100 g castor sugar

25 ml strained fresh lime juice

500 ml strained fresh mango
   purée

100 g liquid glucose

**PASSIONFRUIT ICE-CREAM**

400 g castor sugar

12 large egg yolks

1 litre pouring (35 per cent)
   cream

500 ml Passionfruit Juice (see
   page 10)

This slice of ice-cream and sorbet captures the flavours of summer tropical fruit: I make a play on the commercial iceblock confection of the same name but give it a sophisticated flavour boost and presentation. The flavours and textures are sublime together, but if you don't have the correct moulds or equipment to make it as I have, don't despair! The flavours can be simply layered one upon the other in a rectangular plastic tub and set in the freezer – the taste will be the same. When making ice-cream and sorbet, always choose very ripe fruit at its prime to maximise flavour.

1    To make the pineapple sorbet, whisk the castor sugar into the pineapple juice until the sugar has dissolved. Melt the liquid glucose in a bowl over a bain-marie, then stir it thoroughly into the juice. Churn in an ice-cream machine according to the manufacturer's instructions. Spoon the sorbet into a 32 cm × 5 cm × 4 cm semi-circular mould and freeze for at least 6 hours until firm.

2    To make the mango sorbet, whisk the castor sugar and lime juice into the mango purée until the sugar has dissolved. Melt the liquid glucose in a bowl over a bain-marie, then stir it thoroughly into the purée. Churn in an ice-cream machine according to the manufacturer's instructions until firm.

3    Using a small palette knife, 'paint' a 5 mm layer of the mango sorbet onto the exposed surface of the frozen pineapple sorbet. Return the pineapple sorbet to the freezer for at least 2 hours.

4    Churn the mango sorbet again until firm. Run the pineapple sorbet mould under hot water for a few seconds and turn the sorbet

out onto a foil-lined board. Paint the rounded surface with a 5 mm layer of mango sorbet. Return the moulded sorbet to the freezer on the board for another 2 hours. Freeze the remaining mango sorbet until required again.

5    To make the passionfruit ice-cream, whisk the castor sugar and egg yolks in a bowl until pale and creamy. Bring 500 ml of the cream to simmering point in a saucepan. Whisk the passionfruit juice into the egg mixture, then slowly whisk in the hot cream. Stand the bowl over a bain-marie and cook gently, stirring, until the mixture coats the back of a spoon. Pass the custard through a fine-meshed sieve into a bowl, then whisk in the remaining cream and allow to cool. Churn the cool passionfruit mixture in an ice-cream machine according to the manufacturer's instructions until just firm.

6    Line a 32 cm × 8 cm × 8 cm rectangular mould with baking paper – it should be wider and deeper than the semi-circular mould used for the pineapple sorbet – making sure the paper extends beyond the tin (this will help you remove the ice-cream from the mould later on). Spoon a 2 cm deep layer of

➤

passionfruit ice-cream over the base of the rectangular mould. Freeze for 2 hours until the ice-cream is very firm.

**7**   To complete the ice-cream assembly, churn the passionfruit ice-cream again until firm. Sit the mango-coated pineapple sorbet on the passionfruit ice-cream layer in the rectangular mould, then spoon the remaining passionfruit ice-cream around and over the sorbet until the mould is full. Tap the mould firmly to ensure there are no air bubbles in the ice-cream. Return the mould to the freezer for at least 10 hours.

**8**   Churn the remaining mango sorbet until firm, then remove the mould from the freezer. Paint a 5 mm layer of mango sorbet over the exposed ice-cream surface and freeze again for 2 hours.

**9**   Run the mould under hot water for a few seconds, then turn the ice-cream log out onto a foil-lined board, using the paper lining to slide the ice-cream from its mould. Remove the paper from the ice-cream. Return the log to the freezer on the board for 30 minutes to allow it to firm again. Churn the remaining mango sorbet again until firm, then use it to paint the remaining 3 ice-cream surfaces with a 5 mm layer. Freeze for another 2 hours before serving.

**10**   To serve, cut the ice-cream into 2 cm thick slices using a hot, wet, sharp knife and lie each slice on a cold plate.

# HONEYCOMB, CARAMEL AND BITTER CHOCOLATE ICE-CREAM SANDWICHES WITH CHOCOLATE FLORENTINES

**T**his dessert is immensely popular, since the flavours are universal favourites. The sweetness and richness of the ice-cream layers are countered by the dark and bitter chocolate: it gives a sense of balance to the formula, so that the palate is not loaded with sugar. But for success the chocolate you use must be dark couverture at least 64 per cent chocolate liquor. I use a metal triangular mould but a cardboard mould made to the same dimensions works well too – just remember to line it with baking paper.

**1**   Line a 32 cm x 12 cm x 12 cm triangular mould with baking paper, making sure the paper extends beyond the tin (this will help you remove the ice-cream from the mould later).

**2**   To make the caramel ice-cream, bring the cream and milk to simmering point in a saucepan. Whisk the egg yolks and 150 g of the castor sugar in a bowl until pale and creamy, then whisk in the hot cream mixture. Stand the bowl over a bain-marie and cook, stirring, until the mixture coats the back of a spoon. Set aside.

**3**   In another saucepan, boil the remaining 375 g castor sugar and the water over a high heat without stirring to make a caramel. Add a little of the custard to the caramel as soon as it reaches the desired colour (be careful, it will bubble and expand, so have everything ready!), then whisk the caramel back into the custard. Pass the custard through a fine-meshed sieve into a bowl and allow to cool. Churn in an ice-cream machine according to the manufacturer's instructions. Spoon the caramel ice-cream into the mould until a third full. Freeze for 2 hours until firm.

**4**   To make the honeycomb ice-cream, bring the milk to simmering point in a saucepan.

Whisk the egg yolks and castor sugar in a bowl until pale and creamy, then whisk in the hot milk. Stand the bowl over a bain-marie and cook, stirring, until the mixture coats the back of a spoon. Pass the custard through a fine-meshed sieve into a bowl and allow to cool. Stir the cream into the cooled custard, then churn in an ice-cream machine according to the manufacturer's instructions. When the ice-cream is firm, stir in the honeycomb, then spoon it into the mould until two-thirds full. Return the mould to the freezer for 2 hours.

**5**   To make the bitter chocolate ice-cream, shave the chocolate and melt it in the milk in a saucepan over a low heat until the chocolate has softened completely and the milk reaches blood temperature. Whisk the egg yolks and the castor sugar in a bowl until pale and creamy, then whisk in the hot chocolate milk. Stand the bowl over a bain-marie and cook, stirring, until the mixture coats the back of a spoon. Pass the custard through a fine-meshed sieve into a bowl and allow to cool. Stir the cream into the cooled custard, then churn in an ice-cream machine according to the manufacturer's instructions.

**6**   Fill the mould with the bitter chocolate ice-cream, ensuring the top is smooth and

### CARAMEL ICE-CREAM
1 litre pouring (35 per cent) cream
500 ml milk
12 egg yolks
525 g castor sugar
100 ml water

### HONEYCOMB ICE-CREAM
350 ml milk
4 large egg yolks
150 g castor sugar
350 ml pouring (35 per cent) cream
125 g Honeycomb (see page 135), crumbled

### BITTER CHOCOLATE ICE-CREAM
300 g bitter dark couverture chocolate
500 ml milk
6 large egg yolks
200 g castor sugar
500 ml pouring (35 per cent) cream

### CHOCOLATE FLORENTINES
1 quantity Brandy Snap Biscuit mixture (see page 19)
1 teaspoon minced candied ginger
1 teaspoon minced candied citron
1 teaspoon minced candied pear
150 g dark couverture chocolate

➤

even. You should now have 3 layers of ice-cream of equal thickness. Freeze the mould overnight or for at least 10 hours before turning out.

**7** To make the chocolate florentines, preheat the oven to 180°C and line a baking tray with baking paper. Make the brandy snap biscuit mixture as instructed, then stir in the minced candied fruit. Press 2 tablespoons of the mixture onto the centre of the tray, then cover the mixture with another piece of baking paper and flatten with a rolling pin. Remove the top sheet of paper and bake the biscuit for 6 minutes or until golden. Remove the tray from the oven and allow the biscuit to cool for 1 minute, then cut out triangular biscuits slightly larger than the ice-cream mould. Use a large, sharp knife and cut with precision and firmness. Work quickly before the biscuit cools and sets, when it becomes impossible to cut without breaking. Repeat the process until you have 12 biscuits. Cool the biscuits on a wire rack until firm.

**8** Gently melt the chocolate over a bain-marie. Paint the flat side of the cooled biscuits liberally with the melted chocolate using a pastry brush, then refrigerate the florentines on the rack until the chocolate becomes firm. Carefully remove the biscuits from the rack using a metal spatula and refrigerate in an airtight container between layers of baking paper until ready to use.

**9** Run the mould under hot water for a few seconds, then turn the ice-cream log out onto a foil-lined board, using the paper lining to slide the ice-cream from its mould. Remove the paper from the ice-cream. Return the log to the freezer on the board for 30 minutes to firm again.

**10** To serve, cut the ice-cream into 2 cm thick slices using a hot, wet, sharp knife. Put a chocolate florentine in the centre of each cold serving plate, then sit an ice-cream slice on the biscuit and then top with another biscuit. Both florentines are placed with the chocolate surface facing upwards.

HONEYCOMB, CARAMEL AND BITTER CHOCOLATE ICE-CREAM SANDWICH WITH CHOCOLATE FLORENTINES

CASSATA ICE-CREAM SLICE

# CASSATA ICE-CREAM SLICE

Cassata originates from southern Italy or Sicily and should, by definition, consist of three different ice-creams, one layer including candied fruit and nuts. It is traditionally made in a basin or bombe mould and turned out to be cut into wedges.

Vanilla sugar is made by storing a vanilla bean in a jar of castor sugar – it's a great way to re-use beans and the sugar picks up their flavour wonderfully.

1 Chill a 2 litre domed bowl with a diameter of 26 cm in the refrigerator.

2 Make the raspberry sorbet as instructed, then spread a 5 mm layer over the inside of the chilled bowl using a small palette knife. Freeze for 30 minutes until set.

3 To make the pistachio nougat ice-cream, whisk the egg whites until stiff, then slowly add the castor sugar, as if making a meringue. Make sure the egg whites remain stiff and can hold their shape. Whip the cream until thick, then fold in the crushed praline. Fold the cream mixture into the egg whites, then spread the mixture over the raspberry sorbet layer in the mould to cover it – the mould should be half-full by now. Freeze until firm, about 2 hours.

4 Churn the remaining raspberry sorbet again until firm, then spread a 1 cm thick layer over the pistachio nougat ice-cream. Freeze for 2 hours.

5 To make the candied fruit ice-cream, bring the milk and 375 ml of the cream to simmering point in a saucepan. Whisk the egg yolks and vanilla sugar in a bowl until pale and creamy, then whisk in the hot milk mixture. Stand the bowl over a bain-marie and cook, stirring, until the mixture coats the back of a spoon. Pass the custard through a fine-meshed sieve, then stir in the remaining cream and the candied fruit and allow to cool. Churn the cool custard in an ice-cream machine according to the manufacturer's instructions until firm. Spread the candied fruit ice-cream over the raspberry sorbet layer until 1 cm from the top of the mould, then freeze for 3 hours until firm.

6 Churn the raspberry sorbet again until firm, then spread a 1 cm layer over the surface of the candied fruit ice-cream, sealing the mould completely. Freeze the cassata overnight or for at least 10 hours.

7 To serve, run the mould under hot water for a few seconds, then turn the ice-cream out onto a board and slice it into wedges with a hot, wet, sharp knife. Serve the cassata slice on cold plates.

2 quantities Raspberry Sorbet
  (see page 128)

**PISTACHIO NOUGAT
ICE-CREAM**
250 g egg whites
270 g castor sugar
450 ml thick (45 per cent) cream
½ quantity pistachio Praline (see
  page 29)

**CANDIED FRUIT ICE-CREAM**
375 ml milk
750 ml pouring (35 per cent)
  cream
9 large egg yolks
300 g vanilla sugar
1 tablespoon minced candied
  citron
1 tablespoon minced candied
  orange peel
2 teaspoons minced candied
  ginger

# FREEDOM SORBET SLICE

1 quantity Raspberry Sorbet (see
    page 128)
1 quantity Red Papaya Sorbet
    (see page 113)

**PASSIONFRUIT SORBET**

100 g castor sugar
500 ml Passionfruit Juice (see
    page 10)
100 g liquid glucose

**KIWIFRUIT SORBET**

100 g castor sugar
500 ml strained fresh kiwifruit
    purée
100 g liquid glucose

**BLUE CURAÇAO PINEAPPLE
SORBET**

50 g castor sugar
50 ml blue curaçao liqueur
500 ml strained fresh pineapple
    juice
75 g liquid glucose

**BLACKBERRY SORBET**

100 g castor sugar
500 ml strained fresh blackberry
    purée
100 g liquid glucose

**T**his sorbet construction is very much a folly, making dessert a bit of fun and fantasy. It draws on the freedom flag, a symbol that has come to represent gay and lesbian pride in our community, and each colour is made from a fruit that most closely resembles it. This confection also revels in the title of 'Priscilla – Queen of Desserts', as a tribute to the camp nature of the film. This is, after all, a very camp interpretation of a dessert!

Any leftover sorbet can be frozen for another use. If you don't have a triangular mould, use a rectangular one.

**1**   Line a 32 cm x 12 cm x 8 cm triangular mould with baking paper, making sure the paper extends beyond the tin (this will help you remove the ice-cream from the mould later on).

**2**   Make the raspberry sorbet as instructed, then fill the mould by one-sixth. Freeze the mould for 1 hour until firm.

**3**   Make the red papaya sorbet as instructed, then spoon it into the mould over the raspberry sorbet. The mould should be a third full by now. Freeze for 1 hour.

**4**   To make the passionfruit sorbet, whisk the castor sugar into the passionfruit juice until the sugar has dissolved. Melt the liquid glucose in a bowl over a bain-marie, then stir it thoroughly into the juice. Churn in an ice-cream machine according to the manufacturer's instructions until firm. Spoon the passionfruit sorbet into the mould over the papaya sorbet. The mould should be half-full by now. Freeze for 1 hour.

**5**   To make the kiwifruit sorbet, follow the above procedure, then spoon a layer over the passionfruit sorbet and freeze for 2 hours.

**6**   To make the blue curaçao pineapple sorbet, whisk the castor sugar and blue curaçao into the pineapple juice until the sugar has dissolved. Melt the liquid glucose in a bowl over a bain-marie, then stir it thoroughly into the juice. Churn according to the manufacturer's instructions, then add the next layer to the mould and freeze for 2 hours.

**7**   To make the blackberry sorbet, repeat the above process and add the final layer to the mould. Smooth the surface and freeze for 12 hours or overnight before turning out.

**8**   Run the mould under hot water for a few seconds, then turn the ice-cream log out onto a foil-lined board, using the paper lining to slide the ice-cream from its mould. Remove the paper, then return the log to the freezer on its board for 30 minutes to allow it to firm.

**9**   To serve, cut the ice-cream into 4 cm thick slices with a hot, wet, sharp knife and sit each slice upright on a cold plate.

FREEDOM SORBET SLICE

LEMON VERBENA ICE-CREAM WITH PRALINE TOFFEE WAFERS

# LEMON VERBENA ICE-CREAM WITH PRALINE TOFFEE WAFERS

This is an extremely simple dessert to prepare as it involves only one flavour of ice-cream and the shape of the mould determines the shape of the textured wafers.

Lemon verbena is a wonderfully fragrant and refreshing summer herb that is best cultivated when the tiny flowers appear as they intensify the flavour when the herb is infused in liquid. The leaves can be collected and dried for use in cooking through the year and they also form a refreshing base for a tisane.

100 ml lemon syrup (see Citrus
   Syrup page 8)

### LEMON VERBENA ICE-CREAM
75 g lemon verbena leaves
500 ml milk
6 large egg yolks
200 g castor sugar
500 ml pouring (35 per cent)
   cream

### PRALINE TOFFEE WAFERS
1 quantity Tuile Biscuit mixture
   (see page 18)
4 tablespoons Brandy Snap
   Biscuit mixture (see page 19)
2 tablespoons almond Praline
   (see page 29)

1   To make the lemon verbena ice-cream, infuse the lemon verbena in the milk in a saucepan over a very low heat until simmering point is reached. The slower the infusion, the better the flavour. Whisk the egg yolks and castor sugar in a bowl until pale and creamy, then whisk in the hot milk mixture. Stand the bowl over a bain-marie and cook, stirring, until the mixture coats the back of a spoon. Pass the custard through a fine-meshed sieve into a bowl, then discard the lemon verbena and allow to cool. Stir the cream into the cooled custard, then churn in an ice-cream machine according to the manufacturer's instructions until firm. Fill a 30 cm x 6 cm cylindrical mould with the ice-cream, then press it shut and freeze for at least 8 hours.

2   To make the praline toffee wafers, butter and flour a baking tray and chill it in the refrigerator. Make the tuile biscuit mixture as instructed, then work it on a bench with a palette knife to make it as malleable as possible. Spread the tuile mixture onto the cold tray in a thin, even layer, then chill again until the mixture becomes firm, about 1 hour.

3   Meanwhile, preheat the oven to 180°C. Make the brandy snap biscuit mixture as instructed, then spread it onto a tray lined with baking paper. Cover the mixture with another piece of baking paper and flatten with a rolling pin to make a smooth, thin layer. Remove the top sheet of paper and bake the brandy snap biscuit sheet for 5 minutes until golden. Remove the tray from the oven and slice the biscuit into 5 mm wide strips the length of the tray. Work the biscuit while it is hot and malleable, as it will fracture as it cools. Reduce the oven temperature to 160°C.

4   Bake the chilled tuile sheet for 4 minutes – it should be just set but not coloured. Remove the tray from the oven and lie the brandy snap biscuit strips across the tuile sheet at 1 cm intervals to give a striped effect. Sprinkle the praline over the whole tray. Return the tray to the oven and bake for a further 3 minutes until the tuile starts to colour. Remove from the oven and use a 9 cm round pastry cutter to cut out 12 biscuits. Slide the biscuits onto a wire rack to cool, then store in an airtight container between layers of paper until ready to serve.

5   Remove the mould from the freezer and run it under hot water for a few seconds, then turn the lemon verbena ice-cream log out onto a foil-lined board. Return the log to the freezer for 30 minutes to firm.

6   To serve, put a praline toffee wafer in the centre of each cold serving plate. Cut the ice-cream into 3 cm thick slices using a hot, wet, sharp knife. Put the ice-cream on the wafer, then top with another wafer, making sure that the striped surface is uppermost. Drizzle lemon syrup around the base of each biscuit.

SORBET COUPÉS WITH CIGAR TUILES

# SORBET COUPÉS WITH CIGAR TUILES

I don't usually serve ice-cream or sorbet as scoops, as my work is usually defined by architecture and more complex construction. However, if you have some beautiful serving vessels like the ones pictured, then a simple scoop in each one gives enough form, definition and style to carry it off. Rely on beautiful flavours and perfect texture, churned at the last minute, and you'll have a real winner for a simple dessert. Spend some time perfecting the cigar tuiles as a serious art form – be prepared for burnt fingertips!

I use a saccharometer to measure the baumé level or sugar density of the blood-orange sorbet. It's not an essential piece of equipment as the weights and measures I give here are specific and accurate, but citrus sorbets can be the most difficult as the acid levels in fruit varies, affecting the sugar:acid ratio and the final texture of the sorbet. If the sorbet is too soft or like snow, there is too much sugar; if it is too hard and like ice, there is not enough sugar.

1 quantity Raspberry Sorbet (see page 128)
1 quantity Pineapple Sorbet (see page 114)
1 quantity Tuile Biscuit mixture (see page 18)

**BLOOD-ORANGE SORBET**
750 ml Sugar Syrup (see page 8)
700 ml water
zest of 3 blood oranges
600 ml strained fresh blood-orange juice

1   Make the raspberry sorbet as instructed and freeze for 3 hours before serving.

2   Make the pineapple sorbet as instructed and freeze for 3 hours before serving.

3   To make the blood-orange sorbet, bring the sugar syrup, water and orange zest to simmering point in a saucepan, then allow to cool. Strain and discard the zest. Stir the blood-orange juice into the syrup mixture and measure the baumé level with a saccharometer – it should read 14° baumé. If it reads below, stir in a little extra sugar; if it reads above, add a little water. Churn in an ice-cream machine according to the manufacturer's instructions until firm. Freeze for 3 hours before serving.

4   To make the cigar tuiles, butter and flour a baking tray. Make the tuile biscuit mixture as instructed, then spread the biscuit mixture thinly and evenly over the tray. Refrigerate for 1 hour.

5   Preheat the oven to 140°C. Bake the chilled biscuit sheet for 5 minutes or just until pale golden. Remove the tray from the oven, then cut the biscuit sheet into 18 x 8 cm squares with a sharp knife. Roll each square into a cigar shape, working quickly on the hot tray as the biscuit will begin to set and become less flexible. Allow the cigars to cool on a wire rack, then store in an airtight container until ready to use.

6   For each person, serve a scoop of each sorbet in separate cups with a cigar tuile per sorbet. For a simpler presentation, just serve the scoops in a bowl per person.

# A SLICE OF PRIDE

1 quantity Passionfruit Ice-cream
(see page 114)

**STRAWBERRY ICE-CREAM**
180 g castor sugar
25 ml strained fresh lemon juice
250 ml strained fresh strawberry
   purée
250 ml pouring (35 per cent)
   cream

**RASPBERRY SORBET**
125 g castor sugar
25 ml strained fresh lime juice
750 ml strained fresh raspberry
   purée
150 g liquid glucose

**T**his ice-cream and sorbet construction began as a way of marking the Sydney Gay and Lesbian Mardi Gras festival in February and March each year. The enticing tropical flavours are formed to capture the symbol of gay pride, the pink triangle. It becomes a visual and edible feast of celebration.

**1**   Line a 32 cm × 7 cm × 7 cm triangular mould with baking paper, making sure the paper extends beyond the tin (this will help you remove the ice-cream from the mould later on).

**2**   To make the strawberry ice-cream, whisk the castor sugar and lemon juice into the strawberry purée until the sugar has dissolved. Stir the cream into the mixture and churn in an ice-cream machine according to the manufacturer's instructions. Fill the triangular mould with the strawberry ice-cream, then tap it firmly to ensure there are no air bubbles in the ice-cream. Smooth the surface level with the mould and cover with the excess paper. Freeze for 12 hours.

**3**   Line a 32 cm × 8 cm × 8 cm rectangular mould with baking paper, making sure the paper extends beyond the tin as above. Make the passionfruit ice-cream as instructed, then spoon it into the mould to a depth of 1.5 cm and freeze for 2 hours until very firm.

**4**   Remove the strawberry ice-cream from its triangular mould by pulling on the paper edges. Remove the paper and position the strawberry log on the passionfruit layer in the centre of the rectangular mould. Freeze for 1 hour to firm.

**5**   Rechurn the remaining passionfruit ice-cream, then fill the rectangular mould so that the strawberry triangle is covered (you will have some passionfruit ice-cream left over –

freeze this as a standby dessert). Freeze for 12 hours.

**6**   To make the raspberry sorbet, whisk the castor sugar and lime juice into the raspberry purée until the sugar has dissolved. Melt the liquid glucose in a bowl over a bain-marie, then stir it thoroughly into the purée. Churn in an ice-cream machine according to the manufacturer's instructions until firm.

**7**   Remove the rectangular mould from the freezer, then 'paint' a 5 mm layer of raspberry sorbet over the exposed ice-cream surface using a small palette knife and freeze until set, about 1 hour.

**8**   Run the mould under hot water for a few seconds, then turn the ice-cream log out onto its raspberry sorbet base on a foil-lined board, using the paper lining to slide the ice-cream from its mould. Return the log to the freezer on the board for 30 minutes to allow the edges to become very firm.

**9**   Rechurn the remaining raspberry sorbet again until firm. Remove the ice-cream log from the freezer and paint the remaining 3 ice-cream surfaces with a 5 mm layer of raspberry sorbet. Freeze for 2 hours before serving.

**10**   To serve, cut the ice-cream into 2 cm thick slices with a hot, wet, sharp knife and lie each slice on a cold plate.

A SLICE OF PRIDE

# SMALL SWEET THINGS

**P**etits fours are small mouthfuls of edible luxury that end a meal and provide a final exhilaration for the palate. Perfectly crafted sweetmeats to enjoy with an espresso or a liqueur, their intention is to leave a final impression. Their miniature form requires patience and attention to detail, similar to the craft needed to make canapés. It is food that is born of pleasure, not necessity.

As Anne Willan describes in *Great Cooks and Their Recipes – from Taillevent to Escoffier*, petits fours derive their name from the small ovens that were built for the baking of what became 'the name for an entire family of little cakes and cookies'. These were documented by François La Varenne towards the end of the seventeenth century in *Le Pâtissier Français*, the first comprehensive French work on pastry-making.

This chapter is dedicated to the memory of Betty Harris, mother of my partner, Margie. She had a real love and talent for sweet morsels and her dedication to the craft was at its best at Christmas. Betty would spend two or three weeks making 'those little things you eat after pudding' – small biscuits, chocolate things and slices – accounting for everyone's taste and favourites. She taught me many a trick along the way, gave me inspiration and always encouraged me in my love of food. I think of her every time I delve into this form of cooking.

The following array of sweet, delightful mouthfuls are some of my favourites – they are easy to make and even easier to eat!

# CHOCOLATE PANFORTE

hazelnut oil
200 g shelled hazelnuts
200 g blanched almonds
75 g candied apricots
75 g candied pineapple
50 g candied citron
50 g candied pears
50 g dried figs
240 g plain flour
100 g Dutch cocoa powder
2 teaspoons ground cinnamon
1 teaspoon ground ginger
150 g dark couverture chocolate
175 g castor sugar
250 g honey

The Tuscan town of Siena in Italy is renowned for its palio, the annual horse race in the cobbled town square, and its panforte, a local speciality made with nuts, candied fruit and spices. Different varieties of panforte are served in every espresso bar in the town. The following recipe incorporates chocolate to make it just a little richer. Once made, it keeps in good condition for a fortnight in an airtight container. The edible rice paper needed for this recipe comes in sheet form in small packets under the brand name of Zaano (of Greek origin) and is available at good food stores and some supermarkets.

1   Preheat the oven to 160°C, then grease a 24 cm square cake tin with hazelnut oil and line the base with rice paper. Put the hazelnuts and almonds on separate baking trays, ensuring they are in a single layer for even cooking. Dry-roast the nuts for 5–6 minutes until they are golden and have a pronounced nutty aroma. Rub a few hazelnuts at a time between tea towels to remove the skins. Increase the oven temperature to 180°C.

2   Chop the candied fruit and dried figs into chunks. In a bowl, mix the roasted hazelnuts and almonds, fruit, flour, cocoa powder, cinnamon and ginger.

3   Shave the chocolate into another bowl and stand it over a bain-marie until softened.

4   Bring the castor sugar and honey to a boil in a saucepan and simmer for 5 minutes, then pour this into the fruit and nut mixture with the chocolate and incorporate well. Press the mixture into the prepared tin with wet hands to prevent it sticking.

5   Bake the panforte for 15 minutes. Allow it to cool in the tin, then turn it out onto a wire rack. Cut into portions and store in an airtight container until ready to serve.

# CANDIED GINGER SHORTBREAD

**B**uttery, rich shortbread is one of the delights of the biscuit world. Of Scottish origin, shortbread is traditionally baked in a shallow tin and becomes crisp as it cools. Its texture has that melt-in-the-mouth feeling, made possible by the amount of butter in the mixture. Keep the biscuits in an airtight container at room temperature for a few days only – they are best eaten fresh.

300 g unsalted butter
1 egg
1 egg yolk
300 g castor sugar
2 teaspoons minced candied
   ginger
375 g plain flour

**1**  Heat the butter in a saucepan until it browns and clarifies (when the fat molecules separate from the golden liquid). At this stage it will resemble ghee.

**2**  Meanwhile, beat the egg and egg yolk in an electric mixer until pale and frothy. Pass the hot butter through a sieve, then, with the beaters running, very slowly pour the hot butter into the eggs as if making a mayonnaise. The mixture should be quite stiff at this stage and able to hold its own body.

**3**  Slowly add the castor sugar to the mixture in a steady stream, still beating, then toss in the minced candied ginger. Remove the beaters and gently fold in the flour with a spatula.

**4**  Spread the biscuit dough onto the centre of a buttered baking tray, leaving room at the edges for the biscuit to expand during cooking. Refrigerate the tray for 1 hour to allow the dough to set and become cold.

**5**  Preheat the oven to 160°C. Bake the chilled biscuit dough for 35 minutes until golden and cooked through. Remove the tray from the oven and slice the hot biscuit into squares using a sharp, serrated knife. Allow the biscuits to cool on a wire rack. Store the shortbread in an airtight container until ready to use.

CLOCKWISE FROM TOP: CHOCOLATE PANFORTE, COCONUT WAFERS AND CANDIED GINGER SHORTBREAD

# COCONUT WAFERS

These delicate biscuits can accompany a dessert that includes coconut but they are also wonderful on their own with coffee. The mixture keeps refrigerated for a fortnight and you can bake the wafers as you need them. If you find it difficult to mould them into shape, there is nothing to say they can't be served and eaten flat. The shape is a whim – it does not affect taste.

50 g unsalted butter
45 g liquid glucose
90 g castor sugar
35 g plain flour
15 g shredded coconut

1 Melt the butter and liquid glucose in a bowl over a bain-marie, then stir in the castor sugar, flour and coconut until well incorporated. Allow the mixture to cool.

2 Preheat the oven to 180°C and line a baking tray with baking paper. Roll the cool mixture into small balls about the size of marbles. Press balls of the mixture onto the baking tray about 5 cm apart, then bake for 4 minutes or until golden. Remove from the oven, then leave the wafers on the tray for 30 seconds until they just begin to set. Working quickly using a metal spatula, mould the wafers over a small cylinder or rod (a wooden spoon is fine to use) for 2 minutes until cool and set into shape. Store the cool wafers carefully in an airtight container.

# HONEYCOMB

A sweet confection that has a light-as-air and crunchy texture, honeycomb needs to be stored in an airtight container immediately and consumed soon after making as any contact with moisture makes it sticky and soft.

325 g castor sugar
50 g light honey
125 g liquid glucose
60 ml water
15 g bicarbonate of soda

1 Line a workbench with baking paper. Bring the castor sugar, honey, liquid glucose and water to a boil in a large saucepan. Cook over a moderately high heat until the mixture becomes golden brown, like caramel. Add the bicarbonate of soda and whisk quickly. The mixture will appear like molten lava at this stage – it more than doubles in volume (so make sure you are working in a suitably sized pan). Pour the mixture onto the lined workbench, then allow it to cool and set – this will only take about 15 minutes.

2 Remove the paper, then break the honeycomb into manageable pieces and store it in an airtight container well away from heat until ready to use. To serve as a petit four, break the honeycomb into shards.

# PISTACHIO NOUGAT

250 g castor sugar
125 g light honey
100 g liquid glucose
125 ml water
75 g egg whites
½ teaspoon vanilla essence
400 g shelled fresh pistachio nuts,
   chopped

**A** popular confection of Italian origin, nougat is made with a sweet syrup and beaten egg whites and is flavoured with honey, nuts and candied fruit. It does not cope well with humidity, so needs to be used quickly after it is made or stored in an airtight container. I use Zaano rice paper from Greece when making nougat.

1   Line the base of an 18 cm square cake tin with rice paper.

2   Put the castor sugar, honey, liquid glucose and water into a saucepan and stir over a medium heat until the sugar has dissolved and the liquid glucose has softened, then stand a sugar thermometer in the pan.

3   Meanwhile, beat the egg whites in an electric mixer until stiff peaks form. Bring the glucose mixture to a boil, without stirring, over a medium heat until golden and the temperature has reached 140°C. Remove the pan from the heat immediately and slowly pour the syrup into the egg whites, beating continuously. Stir in the vanilla and the nuts slowly, ensuring the mixture remains stiff.

4   Spoon the mixture into the prepared tin and smooth the surface. Cover with more rice paper, pressing down carefully. Sit a weight on the nougat, then cover and leave at room temperature to set overnight.

5   Next day, remove the weight, then turn the nougat out of the tin and cut it into small squares using a sharp knife. Store in an airtight container until ready to serve.

CLOCKWISE FROM LEFT: ALMOND BREAD, PISTACHIO NOUGAT AND HONEYCOMB

# ALMOND BREAD

200 g egg whites
180 g castor sugar
180 g plain flour
180 g blanched almonds

These crisp, wafer-thin biscuits are baked in the first instance as a loaf, which is then cooled, partially frozen, and sliced before being lightly baked again to give a toasted crispbread texture. Almond bread is fragile and must be stored carefully to avoid breaking – it will keep in an airtight container for a week. You can also make this recipe using hazelnuts that have been roasted and skinned.

1    Preheat the oven to 180°C and line a 32 cm x 8 cm x 8 cm rectangular tin with baking paper. Whisk the egg whites in an electric mixer until stiff peaks form, then add the castor sugar in a slow, steady stream, still beating. Fold in the flour and nuts with a spatula. Spoon the mixture into the prepared tin and bake for 30 minutes.

2    Remove the loaf carefully from the tin and cool on a wire rack, then wrap it in foil and freeze until firm enough to slice, about 1 hour.

3    Preheat the oven to 75°C. Cut the frozen loaf into paper-thin slices using a very sharp knife, then lie the slices in a single layer on a baking tray. Toast the almond bread until crisp and only slightly coloured, about 15 minutes (you don't need to turn them). Store in an airtight container until ready to serve.

# CHOCOLATE TRUFFLES

300 g semi-sweet dark
   couverture chocolate
250 ml thick (45 per cent) cream
30 ml Grand Marnier or a liqueur
   of your choice
Dutch cocoa powder

These classic and elegant petits fours, a serious melt-in-the-mouth experience, are considered by many to be the ultimate confection. Made to resemble the exclusive fungi that are dug from the ground in France, they are essentially richly flavoured chocolate ganache rolled in a high-quality cocoa powder, and are best consumed soon after they are made. An alternative coating for the ganache centre is to roll the balls in melted chocolate.

1    Shave the chocolate into a bowl. Bring the cream to simmering point in a saucepan, then pour the hot cream and the liqueur over the chocolate and stir until combined and glossy. Refrigerate the mixture for 2 hours until firm.

2    To make the truffles, roll the cooled mixture into small balls the size of marbles. Dust with sifted cocoa powder to serve.

# ESPRESSO PROFITEROLES

Choux pastry is a twice-cooked pastry: the mixture is cooked on the stove initially, then it is baked to produce the final result. These little pastries are best eaten the day they are made as they soften quickly, especially after they have been filled with the pastry cream. Instead of icing sugar, a richer topping for the profiteroles would be achieved by swirling on some softened Chocolate Cream (see page 17).

1   To make the espresso cream, bring the two creams to simmering point in a saucepan with the espresso coffee. Whisk the egg yolks and castor sugar in a bowl until pale and creamy, then whisk in the hot cream mixture. Stand the bowl over a bain-marie and cook, stirring, until the mixture is the consistency of thick custard. Remove the bowl from the heat and stand it over ice to cool, whisking constantly. Press plastic film down onto the custard to prevent a skin forming and refrigerate until cold and set, about 1 hour.

2   To make the profiterole pastry, bring the water, butter and castor sugar to a boil in a saucepan. Whisk in the flour all at once and then stir with a wooden spoon over a medium heat for 10 minutes until the pastry is elastic and cooked.

3   Transfer the hot dough to the bowl of an electric mixer and beat on medium speed with a flat beater attachment for 5 minutes.

Add the eggs one at a time, allowing each egg to be well incorporated into the mixture before adding the next. The mixture should be glossy and smooth by now.

4   Preheat the oven to 180°C and line a baking tray with baking paper. Spoon the dough into a piping bag fitted with a small, plain, round nozzle and pipe out dollops of pastry at 2 cm intervals. Bake for 15–20 minutes until the pastries are golden and firm. Break one open to see if it has dried out inside – if it is a little damp, bake the pastries for a few extra minutes. Transfer the pastries to a wire rack to cool completely.

5   To assemble the profiteroles, split one side of each pastry open with a small knife and pipe in some of the espresso cream to fill the centre. Close the pastries and dust with icing sugar before serving. Unfilled pastries can be stored in an airtight container but they are best used within a day.

icing sugar

### ESPRESSO CREAM
250 ml thick (45 per cent) cream
100 ml pouring (35 per cent) cream
25 ml strong espresso coffee
8 large egg yolks
85 g castor sugar

### PROFITEROLE PASTRY
150 ml water
50 g unsalted butter
20 g castor sugar
100 g plain flour
3 large eggs

CLOCKWISE FROM TOP LEFT: CHOCOLATE TRUFFLES, ESPRESSO PROFITEROLES, CHOCOLATE CREAM MERINGUES AND MACAROONS

# MACAROONS

These crunchy biscuits are great on their own, but their texture also lends them to being incorporated into dessert work (see Baked Rhubarb and Hazelnut Macaroon Crumble on page 65 and Almond Macaroon Nectarines with Sauternes Custard on page 102).

250 g flaked almonds *or* whole hazelnuts
250 g castor sugar
50 g egg whites

1   Preheat the oven to 120°C and line a baking tray with baking paper. In a food processor, pulse the nuts and castor sugar until just mixed. Fold the egg whites into the nut mixture, then stir to incorporate.

2   Spoon the mixture into a piping bag fitted with a medium-sized round nozzle. Pipe small dollops of the mixture onto the tray at intervals of 5 cm. Bake for 15–20 minutes or until just set.

3   Remove the tray from the oven and allow the macaroons to cool on a wire rack. Store in an airtight container until ready to serve.

# CHOCOLATE CREAM MERINGUES

A simple and satisfying, not-too-rich chocolate bite to make and serve with coffee. The meringues will keep in an airtight container for a week – just spread them with the chocolate cream as you are ready to serve them. Use the best-quality chocolate for the cream as it will enhance the flavour and texture.

½ quantity Chocolate Cream (see page 17)
1 quantity Meringue mixture (see page 15)
15 g Dutch cocoa powder

1   Make the chocolate cream as instructed, then allow it to set in the refrigerator for about 2 hours.

2   Preheat the oven to 50°C and line a baking tray with baking paper. Make the meringue mixture as instructed, adding the cocoa powder with the icing sugar and cornflour. Pipe the meringue mixture onto the tray in little peaked drops.

3   Cook the meringues until set, about 1 hour. Remove the meringues from the oven and allow them to cool on a wire rack for 30 minutes, then store in an airtight container until ready to use.

4   To serve, sandwich 2 meringue drops together with a little chocolate cream and dust with extra cocoa powder.

# CANDIED ORANGE AND GRAPEFRUIT PEEL

peel from 10 oranges *or*
    grapefruit, including pith
Sugar Syrup (see page 8)
castor sugar

**Y**ou may imagine the task of producing candied peel to be laborious, but it's a fun thing to do when you have some spare time on your hands and an abundance of citrus fruit.

1   Slice the peel into thick chunks, then put it into a large, stainless steel stockpot with plenty of cold water and bring it to a boil. Strain the peel, then cover it with fresh cold water and repeat the blanching process 5 times in all to remove any bitterness.

2   Put the softened peel into a wide-based saucepan and cover it with sugar syrup. Bring the pan to simmering point over a low heat and cook for 1 hour until the peel is translucent. Remove the peel from the pan

and put it on a wire rack in a single layer, then cover it with a cloth and leave in a cool place to dry. This will take a couple of days, depending on the humidity – there should be no visible signs of moisture, otherwise a mildew will form.

3   Roll each piece of dried peel in castor sugar and store in an airtight container. As long as there is no moisture in the fruit or the container, the peel will keep indefinitely. To serve, slice each piece into thin strips.

# CHOCOLATE BROWNIE FUDGE SLICE

½ quantity Chocolate Cream
    (see page 17)
170 g unsalted butter
340 g castor sugar
3 large eggs, lightly beaten
75 g Dutch cocoa powder
1 teaspoon vanilla essence
75 g plain flour, sifted
270 g dark couverture chocolate,
    coarsely chopped

**T**hese rich chocolate morsels are best eaten the day they are made, as their texture changes when refrigerated and they don't keep particularly well at room temperature.

1   Make the chocolate cream as instructed and refrigerate it for 2 hours.

2   Preheat the oven to 160°C and grease and line a 20 cm square slice tin. Melt the butter over a low heat in a saucepan. Whisk the castor sugar into the lightly beaten eggs, then stir in the melted butter, cocoa powder and vanilla essence. Mix in the flour with a spatula, then stir in the chopped chocolate.

3   Pour the mixture into the prepared tin and bake over a water bath for 25 minutes or until just set. Allow to cool in the tin.

4   Turn the brownie slab out onto a chopping board and spread the top with a thin layer of the chocolate cream. Allow the cream to firm for about 30 minutes before cutting the slab into small, elegant squares.

# LEMON SYRUP CAKES

Syrup is spooned over these luscious Mediterranean-inspired cakes after they have been baked, making them extremely moist. While they keep for a couple of days, they are best eaten soon after they have been made. This quantity makes about twenty tiny cakes.

180 g unsalted butter
200 g castor sugar
2 large eggs
270 g plain flour
½ teaspoon bicarbonate of soda
125 g plain yoghurt
minced zest of 2 lemons
50 ml strained fresh lemon juice
75 ml lemon syrup (see Citrus Syrup page 8)

1 Preheat the oven to 180°C and butter and flour 24 x 3 cm pattypan tins. Cream the butter and castor sugar in an electric mixer until thick and pale. Add 1 egg at a time, beating well after each one. Sift the flour and bicarbonate of soda and gently fold into the egg mixture by hand, then fold in the yoghurt, lemon zest and juice the same way.

2 Spoon the batter into the pattypans until three-quarters full and bake for 15 minutes until golden, then remove from the oven.

3 Warm the lemon syrup in a saucepan. Spoon some of the warm syrup over the hot cakes, then allow them to sit in their tray for 5 minutes before transferring them to a wire rack standing over a tray. Spoon more syrup over the cakes as they cool, using the candied zest in the syrup as decoration.

# ALMOND MADELEINES

These small, light-as-a-feather delicacies are of French origin, a traditional tea cake made famous by the writings of Marcel Proust. Madeleines are best eaten as soon as they are made. This quantity will make a couple of dozen tiny cakes.

125 g unsalted butter
4 large eggs
175 g castor sugar
50 g ground almonds
1 teaspoon baking powder
150 g plain flour
icing sugar

1 Preheat the oven to 220°C and butter and flour a madeleine tray. Melt the butter over a moderate heat until it begins to brown, then strain it and allow to cool to room temperature.

2 Whisk the eggs in an electric mixer for a few minutes until thick. With the motor running, slowly add the castor sugar and beat on high speed until the mixture is thick.

3 Mix the ground almonds, baking powder and flour in a bowl, then fold this into the egg mixture by hand, followed by the melted butter. Refrigerate the batter for 30 minutes.

4 Spoon the batter into the madeleine tray until each mould is two-thirds full. Bake for 10 minutes until golden, then remove from the oven and turn out onto a wire rack. Serve the madeleines warm, dusted with icing sugar.

# EQUIPMENT AND INGREDIENTS

Using the right equipment and best ingredients for a dish can mean the difference between success and disappointment.

Most desserts have definition and shape – a created as opposed to natural form. Even a simple cake is dependent on its tin for shape. The more the principles of architecture are introduced, the more the cook has to rely on equipment to achieve the desired result.

But while I have recommended specific pieces of equipment where applicable in the recipes, their use is by no means a blueprint for success. Once you understand the principles and processes behind each dessert, you can then adapt the outcome by using, for example, a different mould. Here I list the pieces of equipment I use regularly and where to find them: familiarise yourself with them and decide which items you need most to carry out the recipes in this book.

In any cooking the end result is determined by the quality of the ingredients with which you start. When making desserts, don't skimp on what you use but go for maximum flavour, even when making pastry or a simple custard. I will go to my grave believing that it is how you eat, the quality of what you eat, that makes a difference to your being.

I describe here some of the less familiar ingredients you may encounter in this book, along with my preferred more everyday items. I urge you to use specific ingredients when they are called for so that you experience each dessert as I first planned it. To do otherwise will compromise the result and possibly disappoint.

# EQUIPMENT

## BAIN-MARIE

A bain-marie is simply a water bath over or in which food requiring gentle handling is cooked in another container. It may be a saucepan of simmering water over which a bowl is stood when making a stirred custard; it may be a baking dish of hot water in which custards are baked. (In the latter case, the smaller dishes stand in hot water that comes two-thirds of the way up their sides.) It may also be a baking dish of hot water that is placed on the shelf below a baking brioche or cake.

## BAKING PAPER

I find baking paper indispensable when making desserts. I use the widely available Glad Bake brand to line tins when making cakes, biscuits and moulded ice-cream to ensure the mixture doesn't stick and the end product is easily removed from its tin, mould or tray.

## BAKING TRAYS

When making biscuits or wafers I use heavy, cast-iron baking trays as they don't buckle when heated to high temperatures. They also maintain heat well after they have been removed from the oven, providing precious time to cut and shape biscuits and so on.

## ELECTRIC MIXER

A good electric mixer is a vital addition to any battery of kitchen equipment since hand beaters don't really do the same job. For domestic use I have a KitchenAid, which seems to have a stronger, longer-lasting motor than some of its competitors. Remember to get an electric mixer with a dough hook as well as the more usual whisk and flat beater and make sure that its motor is strong enough to work brioche or bread dough and the like for the required time.

## FOOD PROCESSOR

A modern kitchen, domestic or commercial, cannot survive without a food processor. There are many brands on the market now, so choose one with a strong motor and a generously sized bowl. I use the industrial-strength Robotcoupe but I also back this up with an electric blender, as I find the blades produce a finer paste. Many food-processor units now come with a blender attachment.

## FRUIT JUICER

When squeezing citrus fruit I use a Hamilton Beach manual juicer as it retrieves the maximum amount of juice possible. This American-made juicer has been designed for heavy-duty use, so it won't break or fall apart like so many of the flimsy domestic versions. With fruit other than citrus, I simply blend it in a food processor and then pass the pulp through a fine-meshed sieve to achieve a smooth purée or juice.

## ICE-CREAM MACHINE

If you make ice-cream and sorbet at home, an electric ice-cream machine is an essential investment as the results are superior compared to handmade frozen confections. An ice-cream machine aerates the mixture while it is churning and freezing it, preventing the formation of ice particles. I use a Simac ice-cream machine at home – restaurants use industrial machines that are made specifically to cope with large amounts.

## MIXING BOWLS

It is important not to use aluminium or tin bowls when working with fruit, eggs or sugar as a reaction occurs, tainting both the colour and flavour of the food. Copper and stainless steel bowls are best for whipping egg whites – a copper bowl is the best of all (a chemical reaction is said to occur, making the whipped whites very stable), but as copper utensils are very expensive stainless steel is a good, all-purpose alternative. Glass bowls are also fine to use.

## MOULDS AND TINS

Sometimes when I look at the quantity and variety of moulds and tins I own, I wonder if I have an addiction! While I don't expect you to have the same sort of collection (mine fills the kitchen and another room), I recommend that you select a few items to give your work greater scope.

I tend to work with metal moulds, and stainless steel wherever possible. Some plastic dariole moulds are suitable for cold desserts but they usually need more heat to extract the contents, which can create havoc with fragile substances.

The **dariole moulds** I use for individual puddings, charlottes and caramelised creams are 120 ml (with a 6 cm wide base), 150 ml (with a 6 cm wide base) and 200 ml (with a 9 cm wide base).

►

While the original purpose of **metal pastry horn moulds** was to act as a support for pastry that would then carry custard or cream, I use them for all sorts of things. I wrap hot tuile biscuits around them when making ice-cream cones, use them as a base for piping meringue into spectacular shapes or fill them with ice-cream to create dramatic 'cones' to up-end on the plate. I prefer to use metal pastry horn moulds that are 12 cm high and 4 cm wide.

For the **moulded ice-creams** in this book, I have recommended using a rectangular mould (in fact, this is simply a loaf tin) of 32 cm x 8 cm x 8 cm, a 32 cm x 5 cm x 4 cm semi-circular mould and hinged cylindrical moulds that are 32 cm x 4 cm and 30 cm x 6 cm respectively. I have also used several triangular moulds, each of which is 32 cm long but of varying widths and heights: 32 cm x 12 cm x 12 cm; 32 cm x 12 cm x 8 cm, and 32 cm x 7 cm x 7 cm. Individual 9 cm high x 8 cm wide pyramid moulds have been recommended in one recipe but can also be replicated in cardboard.

The **cake tins** I use are mostly made of aluminium or are Teflon-coated. Either way, I always line them with baking paper to ensure easy removal of the contents. The cake tins called for in this book are 15 cm x 15 cm; 18 cm x 18 cm; 24 cm x 24 cm; and 24 cm x 20 cm. The slice tins I have used are 32 cm x 24 cm x 4 cm and 20 cm x 20 cm x 3 cm. A rectangular or loaf tin of 32 cm x 8 cm x 8 cm is recommended – look for the type that has collapsible sides held up by pins, making the removal of the cake (or moulded ice-cream) very easy. **Madeleine** and **pattypan tins** are available in varying sizes – the recipes I give make two dozen tiny cakes, so you may need two or more trays.

**Flan tins** can either be Teflon-coated or loose-bottomed for easy removal. The sizes recommended for the recipes in this book are 10 cm or 12 cm (for individual tarts), 24 cm and 32 cm.

## MUSLIN

Bought from any haberdashery, muslin is useful to have on hand for straining fruit purées, custards and the like, or for draining the whey from ricotta, yoghurt or mascarpone. Muslin can be used happily whenever a fine-meshed sieve is called for.

## NON-REACTIVE POTS AND PANS

It is important to use saucepans, frying pans and stockpots made from stainless steel or enamelled cast-iron when cooking with fruit, eggs or sugar as these ingredients react with aluminium and tin, tainting both the colour and flavour of the food. I like to use a 40 cm wide x 20 cm deep enamelled cast-iron braising pan to poach fruit in a single layer. However, any wide, heavy-based non-reactive pan will do just as well, although the fruit may need to be cooked in batches.

## PALETTE KNIVES

These round-ended, blunt knives are handy for spreading soft ingredients. I find a small palette knife especially useful for 'painting' thin layers of ice-cream or sorbet.

## PASTRY CUTTERS

I use both plain and fluted pastry cutters and find 8 cm, 9 cm and 10 cm cutters useful for desserts that 'stack' biscuits, cream and fruit.

## PIPING BAG AND NOZZLES

A piping bag is handy for filling ice-cream moulds and making meringues as well as its more usual job of piping cream, icing and so on. I prefer to use a plain, round nozzle and find 5 mm and 1 cm wide ones useful.

## RICE PAPER

I use edible rice paper when making nougat and the like. I prefer the Greek brand Zaano, available from speciality food shops.

## SACCHAROMETER

A saccharometer is a glass tube about 24 cm long that is used to measure sugar density. I use it when making citrus sorbets in particular, given that the acidity of the fruit can throw out the sugar:acid ratio leaving the sorbet either too hard or too soft (see page 127 for further discussion). To measure the sugar density of a liquid accurately you need at least 2 litres liquid. I prefer to transfer the liquid to a tall jug and then carefully lower the saccharometer into it, allowing it to float until a reading is obtainable. A saccharometer is not an essential piece of equipment, unless you become addicted to making citrus sorbets!

## SCALES

As dessert work demands accurate weights and measurements, a set of reliable scales is essential. Electronic scales that measure in 2 g increments are the most precise ones to use.

## SIEVES

Sieves are used for many different purposes in cooking: aerating flour, extracting tiny lumps from custards, and making fine fruit purées and sauces. A solid conical or chinois sieve is used for general work, while a fine-meshed one produces very smooth, finely textured sauces, custards and purées and is indispensable in dessert work. A rounded sieve, available with varying degrees of mesh, is also a vital piece of equipment for general purposes.

## SILICONE SHEET

A heavy-duty, non-stick silicone sheet can be used in place of baking paper for a variety of procedures from baking biscuits to crisping tart shells. It is very resilient and can be used many times. However, a silicone sheet is very expensive so must be treated with care: don't use knives or sharp objects on it, wipe it clean with hot water only, and store it rolled up to prevent scratching.

## SPATULAS

Metal and plastic or rubber spatulas have multiple uses in any kitchen. I use a large metal spatula to work tuile biscuit mixture until pliable and also for spreading it on a baking tray – its flippy, blunt blade spreads the mixture much more thinly than any other implement. Metal spatulas are also useful for transferring the cooked product from the baking tray to a wire rack to cool. Plastic or rubber spatulas can be used to mix ingredients or to transfer biscuits and the like from Teflon baking trays or silicone sheets.

## WHISKS

While I use the whisk on my electric mixer to beat egg whites, I always use a hand-held balloon whisk when working with custards and the like. Smaller whisks are useful for smaller quantities.

## COOKWARE SHOPS

There are many terrific cookware shops throughout Australia for the domestic and professional market. I have listed a few of the places that stock the sort of equipment I prefer to use, along with a few international outlets just to whet your appetite.

### SYDNEY
**Accoutrement**  611 Military Road   Mosman NSW 2088   Tel. (02) 9969 1031
**The Bay Tree**  40 Holdsworth Street   Woollahra NSW 2025   Tel. (02) 9328 1101
**Chefs Warehouse**  111–115 Albion Street   Surry Hills NSW 2010   Tel. (02) 9211 4555
**The Essential Ingredient**  4 Australia Street   Camperdown NSW 2050   Tel. (02) 9550 5477
**Simon Johnson**  181 Harris Street   Pyrmont NSW 2009   Tel. (02) 9552 2522

**MELBOURNE**
The Essential Ingredient   Prahran Market   South Yarra VIC 3141   Tel. (03) 9827 9047
Minimax   585 Malvern Road   Toorak VIC 3142   Tel. (03) 9826 0022
Scullerymade   1400 High Street   Malvern VIC 3144   Tel. (03) 9509 4003

**ADELAIDE**
Macmont   41–55 Holden Street   Hindmarsh SA 5007   Tel. (08) 8245 6222

**BRISBANE**
Comcater   3/1 Ross Street   Newstead QLD 4006   Tel. (07) 3252 1233

**HOBART**
Habitat   70 Liverpool Street   Hobart TAS 7000   Tel. (03) 6231 0555

**PERTH**
Amano   12 Station Street   Cottesloe WA 6011   Tel. (08) 9384 0378

**PARIS**

Each time I visit Paris these shops are part of my itinerary. They are for the professional cook but also welcome retail trade and offer a wide range of treasures (some I haven't seen elsewhere): copper pots and pans to die for, moulds and tins of infinite variety, china that asks to be taken home and so on. They all ship internationally, if you find you can't possibly carry what you have bought!

MORA   13 Rue Montmartre   75001 Paris   Tel. (1) 45 08 19 24
E. Dehillerin   18–20 Rue Coquillière   75001 Paris   Tel. (1) 42 36 53 13
A. Simon   48–52 Rue Montmartre   75002 Paris   Tel. (1) 42 33 71 65

**NEW YORK CITY**

New York is the best place to visit if a serious dose of retail therapy is what you are after. All the major department stores, such as Bloomingdale's and Macys, have whole areas or floors devoted to the culinary arts. However, the following two shops are particular favourites.

Dean & De Luca   560 Broadway   New York City NY 10012   Tel. (212) 226 6800
Williams Sonoma   1175 Madison Avenue   New York City NY 10028   Tel. (212) 289 6832

**LONDON**
Divertimenti   33/34 Marylebone High Street   London W1U 4PT   Tel. (020) 7935 0689

# INGREDIENTS

## BUTTER

I use **unsalted butter** in all my cooking because it allows me to determine the level of seasoning in a dish. Because salt acts as a preservative, unsalted butter is a fresher product and has a more delicate flavour, but it also has a shorter shelf-life than salted butter. Cultured butter, the premium butter, is also unsalted and is made in the fashion of European butters where an acidic culture is introduced to full-cream milk before it is churned, giving a more distinct and rich flavour. My favourite brand is Girgar, which is made by Bonlac in Victoria.

If your finances can stretch to it, indulge yourself in some of the fresh French butters being imported into Australia. Try the Lescure brand from the Charente region in south-west France – the unsalted cultured butter comes in a gold pack while another flavoured with sea salt from the region comes in a blue pack under the name of 'Sel de Mer' (this is divine with bread).

## CANDIED FRUIT

Candied fruit is simply fruit that has been cooked in sugar syrup until soft and translucent and then dried before being doused in granulated sugar. Citrus fruit, including the fragrant citron, is most often candied, since the thick rind is well suited to the task. While some restaurants candy fruit, I don't necessarily expect you to take up this challenge at home. Instead, there are many terrific products available on the market. Australia's Riverland region is renowned for its dried and candied fruit and many speciality food shops carry these items. Buy candied fruit in small quantities (citron, for example, is best bought in one piece and cut as it is required) and store it in an airtight container in a cool, dry place or the refrigerator.

## COCONUT MILK AND CREAM

**Coconut milk** is made by pressing freshly grated coconut that has been steeped in hot water. It is rich in oil and high in saturated fat. The first pressing gives the thickest milk; repeated pressings give a more diluted milk each time. Now widely available from supermarkets as well as Asian food stores, coconut milk should be unsweetened and have a smooth consistency. **Coconut cream** is the thick cream scooped from the surface of first-pressed coconut milk. This is the richest form of any coconut product and is available tinned or in block form from Asian food stores and most supermarkets.

## COCONUT SUGAR

Made from the sap of the coconut palm, coconut sugar comes in block form and is the colour of toffee. It is also known by its Malay name, gula melaka. I use coconut sugar to enhance and build on the coconut flavour in a dessert but palm sugar (also known as jaggery) can easily be substituted. I prefer the Malaysian Shrimp and Boy brand, which is available from Asian food stores.

## COFFEE ESSENCE

I use French Trablit coffee essence when I need an intense coffee flavour in a dessert. It's available from professional suppliers but good Italian brands can be found in speciality food shops. If neither are to hand, make a very sweet, triple-strength espresso instead.

## COUVERTURE CHOCOLATE

Couverture chocolate is used by professional cooks as it has a higher percentage of cocoa butter, giving it its characteristically smooth, voluptuous texture and taste. If you like and cook with chocolate, don't even contemplate using cooking or compound chocolate. These include so many other additives that they may give a uniform performance in cooking, allowing for mistakes to be made, and the flavour, as with all inferior ingredients, is sadly lacking.

There are several factors that determine the quality of chocolate, which leads us to how chocolate is made in the first place. The pods from the cacao tree are harvested and fermented for a week, then the beans are removed and dried in the sun ready for export to factories. Here the beans are roasted – different beans at specific temperatures and for varying times – and then ground into a paste. Cocoa butter is extracted with the application of heat, leaving chocolate liquor. Sugar, vanilla, lecithin, dried milk powder or extra cocoa butter may be added at this stage, depending on the type of chocolate being made. (Bitter, dark, semi-sweet and milk chocolate are determined by the ingredients added to the chocolate liquor. I do not consider white chocolate to be a real chocolate since it contains no chocolate liquor and has little chocolate flavour as it is mostly made of milk solids and emulsifiers.) Conching, not unlike kneading, is the final process during which the chocolate is stirred for many hours to break down any cocoa butter solids. This process gives chocolate its balance, character and final texture. The length of time the chocolate is conched depends on the quality the manufacturer is seeking – the longer the conching, the better the chocolate.

Good chocolate should break cleanly, have a shiny surface and be velvety smooth in texture as opposed to grainy. Several brands of quality couverture chocolate are available to professional and home cooks alike. Callebaut from Belgium is probably the most commonly used professional chocolate and is available in many varieties coded according to their grades of chocolate liquor and cocoa butter content. Lindt from Switzerland is a fine-quality, high-grade chocolate that is the most common couverture chocolate on the retail market. It was Rodolphe Lindt who developed the refined process of conching at the end of the nineteenth century.

But my favourite couverture chocolate is the French Valrhona, a sublime product that stands apart from the rest in my mind. I like to use Valrhona's Guanaja Grand Cru for cooking and the Manjari Grand Cru for eating. Both are dark chocolate, the former having a chocolate liquor (or cocoa mass) content of 70 per cent with very little added sugar (I use this as I would bitter chocolate). The latter has a chocolate liquor content of 64 per cent and is made from another variety of bean that gives a totally different flavour. I use this whenever a recipe calls for dark semi-sweet chocolate.

►

Whichever couverture chocolate you choose, treat it with the respect you would accord any other luxury food item. Store it in a sealed container away from light in a cool, dry place, not in the refrigerator if possible. If you live in a hot, tropical climate, you will need to refrigerate chocolate, but you may find that it sweats when removed from the cold, which can cause a bloom that will dull the chocolate and give it a grainy texture. Chilled chocolate will also shatter rather than break cleanly.

## CREAM

Different types of cream are now available, and their varying degrees of fat content can affect the cooking and outcome of a recipe. **Pouring or whipping cream** has a fat content of about 35 per cent and is widely available. **Thick cream** with a fat content of 45 per cent is harder to find and is often only available in speciality shops. I use the one made by Bulla – it is a pure cream that is suitable to use in a dish that is to be cooked, such as the caramelised creams in the 'Architectural Offerings' chapter. **Thickened cream**, readily available in all Australian supermarkets, is pouring cream to which gelatine has been added to give it a thicker appearance. This cream will give a satisfactory result if you substitute it for the 45 per cent cream I prefer, but the full, rich flavour will be absent. Demand that your food store starts supplying the real thing, since it is being made for the professional market!

Very thick or **double cream** such as the King Island Dairy variety has a fat content of up to 55 per cent. This cream is great to serve straight from the refrigerator but is unsuitable for cooking as the high fat content causes the cream to split with heating.

**Clotted cream** is made from scalding unpasteurised milk that then forms a clotted layer on its surface. This cream is the most sensational of them all, the queen of the cream world, and needs to be served as is. Its richness and texture are unparalleled and it has a fat content of up to 65 per cent. Two very successful examples are being made in Victoria at present: a fabulous one by Richard Thomas at the Yarra Valley Dairy comes in 300 g wooden trays, perfect for that special indulgence; the Fitzroy Conservatory packages Raymond Le Grand's terrific clotted cream in a similar fashion, and it also comes in smaller jars. Clotted cream originated in Devon and is known there as Devonshire cream where it is made to accompany scones and jam for that well-known tea.

## DUTCH COCOA POWDER

Dark and unsweetened Dutch cocoa powder (so-called in honour of its inventor, Conrad van Houten) is regarded as the premium ground cocoa product. Cocoa powder is produced when chocolate liquor, a byproduct of chocolate-making, is dried and ground. Alkali is added to make Dutch cocoa powder, neutralising acidity and creating a richer, darker product. Valrhona, the French chocolate company, makes an exquisite cocoa powder that is probably the best I have tasted, just like its couverture chocolate.

## EGG WHITES

Since measurements need to be very precise in dessert work, I have listed egg whites as a weight in recipes that require specific quantities (for example, 100 g egg whites). An average egg white weighs around 30 g. I urge you to become used to this method and to being exact when necessary.

## GELATINE LEAVES

A thickening agent made from animal protein (an agar agar alternative is also available), gelatine leaves tend to give a more accurate measure than the powdered form. They are also odourless and tasteless when added to other ingredients, which is why they are most commonly used in the recipes of professional cooks. Gelatine leaves are sold by the sheet and are available from good supermarkets and speciality food shops. The leaves must be softened in cold water for a few minutes until they are pliable and jelly-like and then squeezed of any excess moisture before being stirred into a liquid until dissolved.

## GHEE

Ghee is a form of clarified butter. It has a much higher flash or burning point than butter, making it very useful for food that needs to be cooked at a high temperature. It also lasts extremely well if wrapped thoroughly. Ghee is available from most supermarkets and Asian food stores.

## HONEY

I use light honeys (blue gum honey, for example) in dessert work. Investigate speciality shops or follow roadside signs offering pure local honeys instead of relying on the refined varieties available in supermarkets.

## KAKADU BREAD DATES

Bread date palms thrive in the hot, dry climate of the Kakadu region of northern Australia where they have been introduced. They have a very short season – the dates are picked in September and are available for only two months in very limited quantities since they are quite new to the market. As supply increases, it is anticipated that the dates will become readily available within a couple of years. The advantage of these dates is their freshness, which is evident in their firm flesh. Other fresh dates can easily be substituted for bread dates, such as the Californian medjool, which is nearly double the size. Fresh dates are sweet (about 50 per cent sugar) and the sugar content concentrates as the fruit dries. When bought fresh, dates are best kept refrigerated in an airtight container.

## LIQUID GLUCOSE

A form of simple sugar also known as dextrose, liquid glucose is not as refined or sweet as castor or granulated sugar. It is sold in a dense 'liquid' form at some speciality shops and most chemists throughout Australia. It is used in dessert-making as it inhibits crystallisation and helps food retain moisture; in particular, it gives a smooth and silky texture to fruit sorbets. Light corn syrup, a type of glucose favoured by American cooks, can be used in place of liquid glucose.

## MAPLE SYRUP

Beware the imitations! **Pure maple syrup**, as I've experienced in Canada, has a wonderful smoky flavour and is graded from Fancy or Grade AA through to Grade C, the flavour increasing in strength with each grade. Simply the sap of the maple tree that has been reduced through boiling, maple syrup is quite expensive since its production is labour-intensive. **Maple-flavoured syrup** is mainly made up of a carrier syrup with a little of the pure syrup added for flavouring. I go for pure maple syrup every time.

## MILK

I would dearly love to use beautiful unpasteurised, unhomogenised full-cream milk in all my cooking, but this is not to be, given the stringent laws of our health departments. I believe that hygiene has been taken to such lengths that flavour has been lost along the way. Ask anyone brought up with the taste of fresh milk from the bucket — unless you are lucky enough to live on a dairy farm, this experience is now restricted to those from a bygone era. Instead, we have become so paranoid about the fat content of our food and naturally occurring harmless bacteria that we now produce consumable items that bear little relation to the original raw ingredient. Go to France sometime and taste the butter and cheese made from unpasteurised milk and you'll see what I mean — and the French are not dying in their thousands! Our versions pale into insignificance in comparison.

I only use full-cream milk, albeit pasteurised and homogenised, in all my cooking. Skim milk and diet versions leave me cold — they are food with no soul.

## ORANGE ESSENCE

Orange essence or oil is an essential oil that has been flavoured with the zest from a bitter orange such as a seville or bergamot. It should be used sparingly as it is quite intense and can produce a bitter aftertaste if used inappropriately. I use the American Boyajian brand, available at selected speciality food shops, and keep it in a cool, dark place. Orange-flower water, while not as intense, can be used in place of orange essence quite successfully.

## ORANGE-FLOWER WATER

The blossoms of the bitter orange are steeped in water to produce this fragrant flavouring, used in many Middle Eastern sweetmeat preparations and confections. It is available from speciality food shops and most Middle Eastern pastry shops.

## SAUTERNES

This sweet dessert wine comes from the Sauternes region in western France and is made from grapes infected with *Botrytis cinerea*, a fungus that increases the sugar content of the fruit. Australia makes some very fine examples of botrytis-infected wines and many that rival their French counterparts. We cannot refer to 'sauternes' in this country, given current appellation laws, but I use it here generically. I regularly use Tollana Botrytis Riesling, De Bortoli Noble One Botrytis Semillon, Primo Estate Botrytis Riesling, Lillypilly Noble Muscat of Alexandria and Katnook Botrytis Chardonnay, but this list is by no means prescriptive or prohibitive of other brands. Wine, like food, is a subjective experience, so trust your own palate.

When cooking with wine, choose one that you will also drink with what you have prepared. Don't be cheap and use a second-rate wine in the dish, keeping the decent one for drinking. Good cooking needs a sense of extravagance: the wine chosen indicates how a cook thinks about and approaches food.

## SUGAR

I prefer to use **castor sugar** in all my cooking rather than granulated sugar as its finer texture means that it breaks down more easily and dissolves almost instantly, giving a better result.

Also known as confectioner's sugar, icing sugar is refined white sugar that has been powdered or ground. **Pure icing sugar** forms clumps that need to be worked through a sieve to achieve a smooth powder. **Icing mixture** has had cornflour added to it to keep it smooth but as this will change the texture of what you are preparing, I suggest you work a little harder with the pure form to achieve the best results and flavour.

When I need to use brown sugar, I prefer **dark-brown sugar**. Simply granulated sugar with molasses added to it, this sugar has a higher molasses content than the light-brown variety. **Demerara sugar** is a crystallised sugar that contains a tiny amount of molasses. I like to use it when caramelising the surface of cream or custard tarts.

## VANILLA

The **vanilla bean** is a vital ingredient to have on hand when making desserts, especially custards. Dry used beans and store them in castor sugar to make **vanilla sugar** – you can also remove the beans from the sugar and use them again. Vanilla beans are available widely, with the very best to be found in speciality food shops.

**Vanilla essence** is made from steeping chopped vanilla beans in alcohol and water but even this term can be misleading as the beans:liquid ratio can alter. Look for **pure vanilla extract** in speciality food shops – it is expensive but you only need tiny amounts of it and the flavour is fabulous. What is sold in our supermarkets as **imitation vanilla** has nothing to do, in fact, with the vanilla bean but is chemically derived from a wood byproduct!

## YEAST

Yeast is a living organism that allows fermentation to occur, essential in breadmaking and other baking. I use **fresh compressed yeast** in preference to active dried yeast – but I do so out of habit since it is the one with which I have become most familiar. Fresh yeast, available from some health-food stores, can be kept refrigerated for about two weeks, so buy it as you need it and check the use-by date. You can substitute **dried yeast** in the recipes in this book – just use half the amount recommended for fresh yeast to achieve the right result. If you want to check that the yeast you have is still active, put a little in warm water with a pinch of sugar: it will start to bubble if it is active.

# BIBLIOGRAPHY

Alexander, Stephanie. *The Cook's Companion*. Viking, Ringwood, 1996.

Allison, Sonia. *The Cassell Food Dictionary*. Cassell Publishers, London, 1990.

Blake, Anthony and Crew, Quentin. *The Great Chefs of France*. Marshall Editions, London, 1978.

Blanc, Raymond. *Blancmange*. BBC Books, London, 1994.

Brillat-Savarin, Jean-Anthelme. *The Physiology of Taste*. Penguin Books, Harmondsworth,

   1994 (1825).

David, Elizabeth. Harvest of the *Cold Months*. Michael Joseph, London, 1994.

Davidson, Alan and Knox, Charlotte. *Fruit*. Mitchell Beazley, London, 1991.

Escoffier, Auguste. *A Guide to Modern Cookery*. Bracken Books, London, 1994 (1909).

Grigson, Jane. *Good Things*. Penguin Books, Harmondsworth, 1971.

— *Jane Grigson's Fruit Book*. Penguin Books, Harmondsworth, 1983.

Luchetti, Emily. *Stars Desserts*. HarperCollins, New York, 1991.

MacLauchlan, Andrew. *New Classic Desserts*. Van Nostrand Reinhold, New York, 1995.

Manfield, Christine. *Paramount Cooking*. Viking, Ringwood, 1995.

Remolif Shere, Lindsey. *Chez Panisse Desserts*. Random House, New York, 1985.

Santich, Barbara. *Looking for Flavour*. Wakefield Press, Adelaide, 1996.

Solomon, Charmaine. *Encyclopedia of Asian Food*. William Heinemann, Melbourne, 1996.

Spencer, Colin and Clifton, Claire (ed.). *The Faber Book of Food*. Faber and Faber, London, 1993.

Tannahill, Reay. *Food in History*. Penguin Books, Harmondsworth, 1973.

Time-Life. *The Good Cook* series (*Confectionery* and *Desserts*), chief consultant Richard Olney.

   Time-Life Books, New York, 1978–81.

Toussaint-Samat, Maguelonne. *The History of Food*. Blackwell, Cambridge, USA, 1987.

Visser, Margaret. *Much Depends on Dinner*. Penguin Books, Harmondsworth, 1986.

— *The Rituals of Dinner*. Grove Weidenfeld, New York, 1991.

Willan, Anne. *Great Cooks and Their Recipes – from Taillevant to Escoffier*. Pavilion Books,

   London, 1992.

# ACKNOWLEDGEMENTS

This book has been made possible by the love and support of my partner in life and work, Margie Harris; the vision and driving ambition of my publisher, Julie Gibbs; the meticulous attention to detail and brilliant eye of my photographer, Ashley Barber; the enthusiasm, perception and tenacity of my editor, Caroline Pizzey; and the understanding of perfection and integrity of my book designer, Jo Hunt. It has been a collaborative effort, our shared experience spurred on by the belief that life is too short to eat bad food. This belief is also held by Simon Johnson, of Simon Johnson Purveyor of Quality Foods, to whom chefs and food lovers in this country owe a great debt and whom I thank for his very generous Foreword.

Special thanks go to Tiffany's for lending me plates for use in the photographs: the Brittania cake stand on page 55; the Honeycomb platter on page 68; the Rock cut platter on page 92; the the Limoge Gold Band dinner plate on page 96, and the Frank Lloyd Wright dinner plate on page 100. Damien Pignolet, Tim Pak Poy, Margie Harris and Ashley Barber also allowed me to use their beautiful plates. And thank you to Dinosaur Designs for making the coloured plates on which the ice-cream is presented.

# INDEX

# PARAMOUNT COOKING

*Paramount Cooking* reeks of strong flavours, with no pretty garnishes and no false modesty. It is bold and uncompromising, like the author.

**Jill Dupleix**
*The Sydney Morning Herald*

This is a book for the passionate cook. It is, in a sense, a manifesto of modern Australian cooking. But it is also Christine Manfield's own manifesto: it shows innovation, passion, intensity, pride, breadth of experience.

**Rita Erlich**
*The Age*

*Paramount Cooking* reaffirms Australia's culinary sophistication. This is the most stylish-looking cookbook ever to have come out of this country – perhaps anywhere.

**Cherry Ripe**
*The Weekend Australian*

Christine Manfield has a simple philosophy: 'Life is too short to eat bad food'. This inventive Sydney chef might like to add: life is too short to read bad cookbooks, because … *Paramount Cooking* sets exciting new standards.

**Simon Plant**
*The Herald Sun*

This is the first book to show truly modern eclectic Australian food, food stolen – dare I say plagiarised – from so many cultures (as we are ourselves), and put together with a freshness that is at long last giving us our own recognisably Australian culinary style.

**Ann Oliver**
*The Advertiser*, Adelaide